WHAT PEOPLE ARE SAYING ABOUT

I Had Other Plans, Lord

Every one of us will at some time in our lives encounter dark days. Nick's experience is a compelling picture of how God's mercy and grace helped him deal with a major detour in his journey. His story will be an inspiration to all who read it and provide answers for those who are experiencing their own dark days. The stories woven throughout the book make it a great read.

—DON SODERQUIST
RETIRED SENIOR VICE CHAIRMAN AND CHIEF OPERATING OFFICER,
WAL-MART STORES, INC.

This book is for everyone whose life story has encountered a plot twist—a critical moment that changes everything. Read Nick's story and be inspired!

—LES PARROTT, PhD
PROFESSOR OF PSYCHOLOGY, SEATTLE PACIFIC UNIVERSITY;
AUTHOR OF *SHOULDA, COULDA, WOULDA*

If your heart is injured and your life feels turned upside down, I Had Other Plans, Lord *offers the guidance and encouragement you will need to heal, hope, and turn things right-side up again. In this book filled with biblical wisdom and inspiring stories about courageous survivors, Nick Gugliotti shares how he overcame a serious setback in his life and learned to trust God for wholeness.*

—ALEC HILL
PRESIDENT OF INTERVARSITY CHRISTIAN FELLOWSHIP/USA,
AUTHOR OF *JUST BUSINESS*

I HAD OTHER PLANS, LORD

How God Turns Pain Into Power

NICK GUGLIOTTI

 LIFE JOURNEY®

Bringing Home the Message for Life

COOK COMMUNICATIONS MINISTRIES
Colorado Springs, Colorado • Paris, Ontario
KINGSWAY COMMUNICATIONS LTD
Eastbourne, England

Life Journey® is an imprint of
Cook Communications Ministries, Colorado Springs, CO 80918
Cook Communications, Paris, Ontario
Kingsway Communications, Eastbourne, England

I HAD OTHER PLANS, LORD
© 2006 Nick Gugliotti

Published in association with the literary agency of Les Stobbe, 300 Doubleday Rd., Tryon, NC 28782.
For more information about the author go to: www.nickgugliotti.com.

The Web site addresses recommended throughout this book are offered as a resource to you. These Web sites are not intended in any way to be or imply an endorsement on the part of Cook Communications Ministries, nor do we vouch for their content.

Cover Design: Two Moore Designs/Ray Moore

First printing, 2006
Printed in the United States of America

1 2 3 4 5 6 7 8 9 10 Printing/Year 10 09 08 07 06

Unless otherwise noted, all Scriptures are taken from the *New American Standard Bible*, © Copyright 1960, 1995 by The Lockman Foundation. Used by permission. Scripture quotations marked NIV are taken from the *Holy Bible, New International Version*®. *NIV*®. Copyright © 1973, 1978, 1984 by International Bible Society. Used by permission of Zondervan. All rights reserved. Scriptures marked NKJV are taken from the New King James Version. Copyright © 1982 by Thomas Nelson, Inc. Used by permission. All rights reserved. Scriptures marked NLT are taken from the *Holy Bible, New Living Translation*, copyright © 1996. Used by permission of Tyndale House Publishers, Inc., Wheaton, Illinois 60189. All rights reserved. Italics have been added by the author for emphasis.

ISBN-13: 978-0-7814-4304-3
ISBN-10: 0-7814-4304-0

LCCN: 2005937772

To every person who has faced or is facing a major and potentially devastating circumstance. My sincere desire is that it may be of some comfort to you. I pray you find the peace and guidance that only God, through our Lord Jesus and his Holy Spirit, can bring

With love to the three people who continue to make my life worth living: my wife, Dawn, my son, Nicholas, and my daughter, Danielle

God has made me fruitful in
the land of my affliction.

—Genesis 41:52

CONTENTS

ACKNOWLEDGMENTS

Many people have helped me learn through the difficulties and challenges of my life. I'd like to acknowledge a few:

My mother, Mary, who has always demonstrated such love for me that I could never feel totally alone.

My brothers and sisters in the community of faith known as Calvary Life Christian Center—especially Pastor John and Carmela Muratori. Ken Richard, my first real pastor, who gave me a foundational understanding of the Bible. George Toles, who has affirmed the value of this book. Diane and

Rocco Gugliotti, who generously let me use their cottage as a writing getaway. My brothers and sisters at The Bible Church, who walked through the valley with me. The wonderful brothers and sisters at Frontline Ministries who supported me with their prayers.

Les Stobbe, my literary agent, who believed in this work and encouraged me to pursue it. Donna, Joe, and Tom of the Worx Group who helped and encouraged me. My editor at Life Journey, Mike Nappa, whose suggestions significantly improved the book.

My wonderful wife, Dawn, who understands how important this book is to me. My children, Nick and Danielle, who continue to inspire me.

INTRODUCTION

Several years ago, my life took a sudden and unexpected turn. I went from a respected executive on the rise to an unemployed "nobody" battling a serious illness. The illness, although potentially terminal, didn't kill me. The heart-wrenching, soul-challenging battle to discover myself almost did. I had to unearth the true self that was left within me after losing the position in society that had previously defined me. Disability insurance and a buy-out agreement made it possible to care for my family, but caring for my devastated self-image was another story.

Some time before my fall, a bridge collapsed in Fairfield County, Connecticut. I remember seeing pictures of the gaping hole where the middle of the bridge had once been. Little did I know that I would experience a collapse and a gaping hole every bit as devastating to me. I was traveling along in the fast lane, with the future mapped out clearly, when the road suddenly gave way beneath me, and I found myself being plunged into an unexpected and undesired place—and I didn't like it one bit.

> ℃
>
> WITH A GRACIOUS GOD AT MY SIDE, I BEGAN TO DISCOVER NEW THINGS ABOUT THIS GIFT WE CALL LIFE.

The road I've traveled since has been full of sharp turns, dips, tortuous climbs, fitful starts, and sudden stops. It has also been full of opportunity. At first I saw none of the opportunity—only the loss. As I experienced one transition after another, I realized there was much to be learned about life, purpose, and faith. With a gracious God at my side, I began to discover new things about this gift we call life.

As one of the counselors at my church, I began to see a pattern in the lives of many of the people who came there for help. Some came because their

marriage had fallen apart, others because they had
lost children to terminal illness. Some were suddenly alone after thirty or forty years of marriage;
others had lost a career. The one thing they all had
in common was the fact that a sudden change in
circumstance had thrown their world into turmoil.

As I began to put the pieces of my own frac-
tured life back together, I saw that perhaps God
had guided me through the process so I could offer
a hand to those facing a similar path toward recovery. These are the people I wrote this book for. If
you are one of them, I want to tell you that no
matter how dark it seems, how lonely you feel, or
how terribly grief may be tearing you apart, "the
God of all comfort" is able to take you through to
joy and peace (2 Cor. 1:3). I know. I have received
his grace and love, and it has allowed me to find my
way again.

Many times during my ordeal I thought, *Lord,
just knock me out 'til it's over.* But he doesn't work
that way. He won't knock you out, but he will
travel the road with you—if you ask him to. I pray
that this book will help you do so.

One Call
Changed It All

⌒

It is not necessary to change. Survival is
not mandatory.

—W. Edwards Deming

Welcome. If you picked up this book or if someone gave it to you, there's a chance that your life, like
mine, has suffered some big change that has you wondering who you really are. Whether it's illness,
disability, loss of a relationship, or some other sudden
change—you and I have some things in common.
Maybe you've been forced to deal with a harsh reality,

and your understanding of who you are is uncertain. It's unsettling to find your world redefined by circumstances, but it happens all the time. For me, it was debilitating illness that wiped out my idea of who I was and where I was going. For you, it may be a different kind of abrupt change. It doesn't matter what caused it—the effect is the same.

> ᢒᢣ
>
> MY JOURNEY
> BEGAN WITH A
> PHONE CALL FROM
> A DOCTOR.

My journey began with a phone call from a doctor.

ᢒᢣ

"Hello," my wife, Dawn, said. "Yes, hi, Dr. Milton ... ah ... uh ... yes, but what does that mean?"

I looked up over the newspaper. As the color drained from Dawn's face, I shivered involuntarily. Dr. Milton wasn't delivering good news, that was apparent. I watched my wife falter under the weight of his words.

"Yes," she said. "Of course, Doctor. We'll be there. Wednesday at two thirty. Thank you, Doctor."

As she hung up the phone, my wife sagged against the clean white trim that framed the opening between our family room and kitchen. I dropped the newspaper—other news had my attention.

"Dawn? What did he say?" I asked.

She wiped her eyes and slowly turned to face me.

"The biopsy shows you have active scarring of your liver. He wants to talk to us about treatment."

"Oh," I said, trying to digest her words, but reacting more to her body language.

Dawn walked over and sat next to me. Her hands trembled. She could barely see me through the blur of her tears. Her hands found my shoulders, and she pulled me toward her. Then quietly I asked, "Is it that serious?" She choked out the words, "I don't know." I felt cold even though she hugged me. "He thinks you should consider leaving work for a while."

> OUR ESSENTIAL VALUE ISN'T DEFINED BY OUR ACTIVITIES, OUR SUCCESSES, OR OUR FAILURES. IT'S NOT EARNED; IT'S GIVEN TO US BY GOD.

At age forty-three, I was president of a successful marketing-communications company. Our finances were stable, and my family was doing well. Opportunities surfaced at every turn; the future looked bright.

I had been an elder in my church for more than fifteen years. I was called upon to preach regularly and was actively involved in our counseling ministry. I had even filled in for a year as associate pastor.

ONE PHONE CALL HAD EXPLODED MY SENSE OF STABILITY.

At age forty-four, I ran into a brick wall—serious illness made it impossible for me to work. Without work, I was no longer sure of my worth. As my confidence slipped away, I began sliding down a very steep hill. That's when four little words—twelve letters—began to haunt me: *Who are you now?*

What we do does not determine who we are. Our essential value isn't defined by our activities, our successes, or our failures. It's not earned; it's given to us by God. Yet many of us spend our lives trying to prove we're acceptable, valued, worthy.

I was no different. I kept asking myself, *What's left without the things you thought made your life valuable? What good are you now that you've lost your place in the world?*

You may be asking yourself similar questions. We all do—sooner or later. It usually happens in times of dramatic change, when we realize there's no easy way out. It's the time we crash into unfiltered reality. It's also when we come face-to-face with God.

Is something forcing you to give up your old life and start over? You can't do it on your own, but you can with God's help: "Now to Him who is able to do far more abundantly beyond all that we ask or think, according to the power that works within us" (Eph. 3:20).

℘

And so began the end of my life—at least as I knew it.

After that short phone call, my reality began to crumble. One phone call had exploded my sense of stability. Things had changed. A major dismantling process had begun.

It wasn't a shock to hear I was sick; I'd known that for some time. It was a shock to find out *how* sick I was. Also, it was unsettling to think I might have

> ℘
>
> DAWN AND I GLANCED AT EACH OTHER. WAS THIS A VISIT FROM THE GHOST OF CHRISTMAS FUTURE?

to leave the business I'd built from its infancy. It meant leaving a lifelong dream. That was hard—very hard.

I had held a job from the day I turned sixteen: from shoe salesman to mason tender; from truck driver to construction worker; from intern to public relations assistant; from sales manager to marketing manager; and from executive to entrepreneur. All through my life I had been taught to see value in any kind of honest work.

In my family, two things violated an unwritten code: (1) bringing shame to the family, and (2) being unwilling to work. For a family of hardworking immigrants, not working was a sin. I didn't realize, at that point, that I was about to become a "sinner."

∽

Two days after Dr. Milton's call, Dawn and I sat in his waiting room. As we idly flipped through magazines, a man entered the office. His wife and daughter fussed with his coat and gloves. His breathing was labored as he steadied himself on his wife's arm. His eyes were set deep, and his cheeks were drawn. His neck looked childlike in a shirt at least two sizes larger than it needed to be.

Dawn and I glanced at each other. Was this a visit from the Ghost of Christmas Future?

"Mr. Gugliotti?" the nurse called out.

"Yes. Here we are," Dawn answered.

"Hello," the nurse said over her shoulder as we followed her down the narrow hall. "How are you today?"

"Fine," I said. She didn't really want a serious answer. In her line of work, caring can be dangerous.

"Okay, step up on the scale for me," she directed. "Good, now follow me, please. Have a seat on the table so I can get a quick blood pressure."

I nodded and followed orders. I was definitely not in control, and it made me nervous.

"Okay, Mr. Gugliotti. Please strip down to your undershorts and put on this johnny coat. The doctor will be in shortly."

An involuntary shudder ran up my exposed spine. Was I having my ticket punched for a trip I didn't want to take? Where was I going? Why did the world suddenly feel so threatening? Why did I feel so small? Was this really happening?

"Hello, Mr. and Mrs. Gugliotti," Dr. Milton said with a smile. He held a file marked "Gugliotti" in his left hand and extended his right hand in greeting. His face glowed with kindness, but deep lines at the corner of his eyes betrayed a weighty share of disappointment.

Dr. Charles Milton had been worn down from years of watching people struggle with serious illness.

He'd had his moments of triumph, but he'd been disappointed more times than he cared to remember.

He made a few jokes to lighten the mood and asked a few questions about fatigue and joint pain. Then he put down the file and rolled his backless chair closer.

> ∞
>
> HE SPOKE IN MEASURED LANGUAGE, THE KIND MOST DOCTORS HAVE LEARNED OVER YEARS IN PRACTICE.

"Doc, what exactly is going on?" I asked.

He crossed his legs and folded his hands over his knee. "Everyone is different, so it's hard to be definite on some of this," he said. "I've had patients with less significant disease do very poorly. I've had patients with more advanced disease respond very well. This is not exact science."

"I understand," I responded.

"Here's your situation. You have hepatitis B and hepatitis C. Based on your records, you've had it for close to thirty years. The biopsy indicates active virus. Frankly, I'd hoped it would come back persistent but not active. There's a big difference. There are many people walking around with a persistent, chronic virus in their system. They're only in danger if the virus converts to an active process. They have no scarring and no liver damage. At some point, your virus became active and began damaging your liver. You have moderate damage, but you will have more. Are you with me so far?"

I nodded slightly.

"The wild card is that no one knows how fast the disease will progress. Worst case, it moves rapidly, and in a year you have hepatomas, tumors on the liver, and you're in serious trouble. Or, your liver could become so damaged you need a transplant. Best-case scenario, it progresses slowly, and the treatment kills off the virus before more damage is done."

"Which way do you think it will go, Doc?" I asked.

"I wish I knew." He spoke in measured language, the kind most doctors have learned over years in practice—careful not to take away hope but not promising anything they can't be sure of. "You could be relatively fine for a year, five years, even fifteen years. You could be very sick very soon. I just don't know. And you have another complication."

"I do?"

> ☞
>
> I SENSED GENUINE COMPASSION—AND THAT SCARED ME EVEN MORE THAN ANYTHING HE HAD SAID.

"Yes. The blood work and the records from at least two specialists indicate you have an ongoing problem in your immune system. Could be from thirty years of fighting a chronic illness. Could be unrelated. The fact is, you aren't able to fight this illness as well as someone who doesn't have a compromised immune function. You're not in the best shape to fight the disease, and the therapy, which isn't easy, will probably be much harder on you."

"Anything else?" I asked.

"Isn't that enough?"

"What's next?" I asked.

Dawn shifted in her chair, her face blank and her heart breaking. Leaning forward to hear every word the doctor said, she managed a labored smile in my direction.

"We start you on the interferon/ribavirin combination as soon as possible," he said. "You'll take three injections per week and six pills every day—and you have to make a decision."

"About what?" I asked.

"About work," he said. "The therapy has some nasty side effects, and it may be quite a bit harder for you. You may become depressed. You may get headaches. You'll almost definitely get flulike symptoms, and you'll probably experience muscle and joint pain. And there's one more thing." He paused.

"You'll probably have to deal with extreme fatigue."
He leaned forward, and our eyes locked. Call it
instinct, intuition, I don't know what, but I sensed
genuine compassion—and that scared me even more
than anything he had said.

"For you, it may be disabling exhaustion. There's
no way to know for sure. But it's safe to say, in your
case, chronic exhaustion is
almost definite."

"So, you're saying I won't
be able to work?" I asked.

"Well, some people are able
to work while on the treatment.
Especially those who don't have
an active virus. But in your case,
I'd advise against it. According
to your wife, you work ten
hours a day, often six days a
week. She told me lately you've
been absolutely drained by the end of the day."

"It's not easy to run a business," I said.

"I know, and I'm not knocking hard work. But
stress is an enemy to the human body. Right now,
your body doesn't need more enemies. On top of
that, your bouts of extreme fatigue are coming more
frequently—and you haven't even started taking the
medicine that will cause considerably more exhaustion.

I DESPERATELY
WANTED TO TURN
BACK TIME—TO
MAKE THE WHOLE
NIGHTMARE GO
AWAY.

You ended up in the emergency room a few months ago, and your wife tells me you're getting migraine headaches. Do you want more reasons?"

"No. I get the point." I knew he was right. It was getting harder every day, and I was pushing myself most of the time. "So what should I do?" I asked.

"Consider a leave of absence. Give yourself at least nine months; maybe twelve months would be better. Take that time to rest and concentrate on getting through the therapy. When that's behind you, you'll be in a better position to consider your future," he said.

> ℘
>
> WELCOME TO THE
> JOURNEY—YOU
> MAY BE ABOUT TO
> OPEN THE DOOR
> TO YOUR SOUL.

My motivation for working hard had always been my family. It would make no sense to push myself now and not be with them later.

I imagined my son, Nicholas, telling his son he wished he could have met me, his grandpa. I visualized a small boy, my grandson, playing soccer. It hurt to see the picture without me in it. I saw my daughter, Danielle, in a beautiful white gown, walking down the aisle with her brother because Dad wasn't there to walk with her. And I saw my wife, Dawn, at the beach, the place we hoped we'd spend our final years together. Instead of shared joy, she carried a heavy weight of memory and loneliness. She walked head down, the mournful cry of a solitary seagull echoing in her ears.

It was so hard. I was afraid. I was uncertain. I couldn't see any option that appealed to me. A character in a novel I once read described this kind of experience as coming to a point in life when you realize the stakes have suddenly changed. The carefree ride of your life screeches to a halt; all those years of bouncing along, life taking you where you want to go, abruptly end. It was that kind of moment for me, and I desperately wanted to turn back time—to make the whole nightmare go away.

"Do you want to take a few days to think it over?" he finally asked.

"Ah, yeah—"

Dawn finished the sentence for me, "Thank you, Doctor. We'll pray about it. We want to do whatever …" her voice cracked. She cleared her throat. "… whatever it takes for him to get better."

For a second I thought I could will it all away. *I don't have to accept this,* I thought. *I'll fight my way through like I always have.*

A stabbing pain in my head brought me back to reality. A migraine headache was on the way.

I didn't know God was moving closer to me as my need increased. I certainly didn't know the call from the doctor's office would turn out to be an invitation from God. How could I know it was the beginning of a very close look at my life and all that I considered important?

Everyone who discovers the difference between being and doing finds peace that God alone can give. If some life-changing event has happened to you, maybe you aren't doing the things you used to, but there are new things you can do. It's hard, but it's the only way. Stop for a second. Take a breath and push aside your busy thoughts. Now, in his presence, ask yourself, *Who am I, really?* The doing naturally follows the being. But first you must discover who you are *now*. It's not easy. I know. But it can be done, because he has promised to help you.

Welcome to the journey—you may be about to open the door to your soul.

> Do not work for the food which perishes, but for the food which endures to eternal life, which the Son of Man will give to you, for on Him the Father, God, has set His seal. (John 6:27)

Why Start Over?

Even though you may want to move forward in your life, you may have one foot on the brakes. In order to be free, we must learn how to let go. Release the hurt. Release the fear. Refuse to entertain your old pain. The energy it takes to hang onto the past is holding you back from a new life. What is it you would let go of today?

—Mary Manin Morrissey

Dawn and I were heading to one of our favorite coffee shops around six o'clock on a Sunday evening. As we exited the highway and came to the light at the bottom of the ramp, a man in his mid-thirties was standing at the median, head down, cardboard sign in hand. I couldn't read the sign, but something about his expression looked sincerely broken. I proceeded to the next light without saying a word to Dawn. I turned left and halfway down the block asked her, "Did that guy look sincere to you?" She said yes. I turned around. Pulling into an adjacent parking lot, I stopped the car and got out. I motioned for the man to come over. He came running.

> I ASKED HIM IF I COULD PRAY FOR HIM, AND HE SAID, "OH, YEAH. PLEASE PRAY FOR ME. I NEED IT BAD."

My mind was clicking on two tracks. On one hand, compassion for another human being was front and center. On the other, I knew an expert manipulator might play me for a fool. He thanked us profusely for stopping. I asked him how he'd gotten to this place. He said he had walked over from the homeless shelter on Benedict Street. I stopped him and said, "No, how did you get to this place in your life? How did you come to be standing on a street corner with a cardboard sign in your hand?"

He said his wife had died three years earlier, and he never could get over it. He'd never been able to start over. Instead, he just lived one day to the next, always avoiding the hard choices that might turn things around. I asked him if he couldn't see himself in a better place. He said he really wanted to. I asked him if I could pray for him, and he said, "Oh, yeah. Please pray for me. I need it bad." He leaned on the car door. Dawn reached through the open window to put her hand on his, and I stood beside him with my arm around his shoulder. As I implored God to touch this man, he interrupted me. "Please ask him to help me like myself! Please. Please."

That's when I realized he didn't think he was worth the space he took up. He hated what he saw in the mirror and spent most of his time sabotaging his own life. It had led him to the streets with a cardboard sign and nothing but the clothes on his back. He didn't see any point in starting over—he didn't even think he *could* start over. He had given up.

Could he have made different choices? I believe he could have. Personally, I believe it grieves God's heart when someone suffers the way this man had, but justice requires every person to be responsible for personal choices. "Let him truly turn to God for help and commit to following our Lord and see what happens." That was and is my prayer for the man with the cardboard sign.

∽

Why start over? We all have to answer that question when important things go wrong. *Why should I make the effort?* you may ask. Here's the honest answer: because you'll live a life of disappointment and despair if you don't. You'll get stuck and stay stuck. You'll rob yourself of the opportunity to be happy again and cut off the good things that lie ahead.

> ∽
>
> WHAT HAPPENS NEXT DEPENDS SOLELY ON THE CHOICES *YOU* MAKE.

There's no denying that unanticipated and unwanted changes are painful. You may have had things all mapped out, and now it's obvious your life won't be the way you thought. That hurts. But here's a foundational principle for starting over: *The quality of your life is based on the choices you make.*

You may have every reason to feel sorry for yourself. Circumstances may seem totally unfair—

and they may well be. And yet, the bottom line is that what happens next depends solely on the choices *you* make. I know, because I didn't make all the right ones and it cost me. But I'll tell you more about that later.

Choice is central to God's plan for mankind. He bestowed on us humans the respect and the dignity that come with free choice. In effect, God says to each one of us, "I know you can learn to choose wisely. But *you* must do the choosing." We can't avoid the consequences of our choices. We can't choose evil and expect good to come. And we can't avoid choosing, because avoidance, in itself, is a choice. It's giving up. Going with the flow only leads to deeper waters.

So, you're in a tough place. You want things to get better. Then you have to come to grips with the fact that you alone are responsible for the next chapter of your life. I'm not saying it's easy. I'm not saying I do it right all the time either. But we have the freedom to choose and therefore the freedom to shape the outcome of our individual lives.

> IF YOU FOCUS ON THE PAST, YOUR MIND WILL STAY THERE IN PAIN AND ANXIETY.

The ABCs of Starting Over

Allow the past to stay in the past. Respect the fact that no one has ever changed history. You simply can't go back. Don't put any more time into things you can't change. Replaying what might have happened won't change it. You can imagine a hundred different ways the situation could have worked out, but, in the end, it won't change anything. And it distracts you from the task at hand—making choices that will move you ahead.

Each new morning brings an opportunity to go backward or go forward. If you focus on the past, your mind will stay there in pain and anxiety. If you ask God to help you look to the future, your mind will begin healing.

Beware of people who won't help you look ahead. Sometimes it's easier to listen to people who allow us to feel sorry for ourselves—but the people who'll help you most feel empathy but know that forward is the only direction you should be going. You need people around

> WHAT'S THE DIFFERENCE BETWEEN SOMEONE WHO HANDLES DISAPPOINTMENT WELL AND SOMEONE WHO DOESN'T?

you who have learned that life is all about adapting to change and the adventure of starting something new. Those people will empower you. The other kind will grease the walls of the pit you'll slide into.

Choice—it's the bottom line. Before every important decision, ask yourself, *Will this choice bring me closer to where I want to go or move me farther away from it?* Ask God's Holy Spirit to help you. He will. It's a promise—and God doesn't break promises. First Kings 8:56 says, "Blessed be the Lord, who has given rest to His people Israel, according to all that He promised; not one word has failed of all His good promise." He's not out to deny your joy, but you must choose wisely in order to find it in its truest form.

> THE INESCAPABLE TRUTH IS THAT GOD WILL WORK IN ANY CIRCUMSTANCE.

The first choice must be to deal honestly with reality. Commit to the facts. They are what they are. An honest appraisal is the only place to begin.

If a relationship has ended, you have no choice but to let it go. By definition it's no longer a relationship. It's fruitless to hang on to the "memory" of something that ended badly. The important thing is to accept that it's over. If you've suffered a financial loss, you have to get past "what might have been": *If only I hadn't invested in that company. If only I hadn't taken a chance on such a risky business proposition.* If you've lost a career, you have to move on. The years you spent in that endeavor are gone—and, who knows, you could find work you love much more.

What's the difference between someone who handles disappointment well and someone who doesn't? Is it that the first person doesn't feel pain and discouragement? Absolutely not! The difference is that the first person chooses to fight for tomorrow, refusing to let the changed circumstance end hope. Even if you're only moving forward in baby steps—that's okay. At least you're getting closer to where you'd like to be.

Again, I'm not saying it's easy. And it certainly requires God's grace and help. But the first step is a choice: to believe that your life *can* get better, that there's good reason to push on. Accept that God says you're important enough for Jesus Christ to die for you. God always has his loving eye on you: "I will instruct you and teach you in the way which you should go; I will counsel you with My eye upon you" (Ps. 32:8).

In the end the choices are ours, and they determine the outcome of our lives. Sometimes we choose wisely and benefit. Sometimes we choose to believe that circumstances have rendered us worthless, and we suffer because of it. We must take stock, pray to God for help, and put one foot in front of the other—slowly but surely moving on—or let the circumstance completely overwhelm us and cause us to make choices that compound the difficulty.

ℰ

STARTING OVER IS ALWAYS AN OPTION.

In the Bible, we see that God is just and gives every person the ability to choose wisely. That's why some individuals who started life in the most difficult circumstances turn out to be incredible people, and others who have everything given to them turn out to be horrible human beings.

The inescapable truth is that God will work in any circumstance. He proves it again and again. He does, however, require willing coworkers—us. He promises to work alongside each one of us, step by step. But we must reach out for the help. We must choose to believe, trust, and stand firm. There's evidence of what can happen all around us. The question is, are we willing to look at it?

There are people like Joni Eareckson Tada, paralyzed in a diving accident when she was a young woman, who chose not to give up. For her, starting over was a monumental task. But with God's help she has lived a life that by any standard is full of purpose and meaning.[1]

I know a pastor who came through a wild lifestyle of drug abuse and immoral living. An accident forced him to reevaluate his life. Today he leads a congregation of young, enthusiastic Christians. Because he took the opportunity to start over, he's helping many others do the same.

I know a woman who nearly drank herself to death. Today, she's a beacon of hope to alcoholics in our community. Her knowledge of the Bible coupled with her genuine love for others puts her in a unique position to tell others how she learned to start over. Many who are trying to do the same rely on her wisdom, love, and availability.

I know a man who was forced out of a job due to consolidation. He had always thought he would retire from that job. When the layoff first happened, his world and his self-confidence were shaken. Today, because he was willing to do the hard work of starting over, he's one of the happiest men I know. He works in the prison system, helping others find strength and determination to start over. He makes less money, but he's full of life because he knows his work matters. The job he held before his layoff doesn't even cross his mind anymore.

Although it's rarely easy, starting over is always an option. It's always a chance to learn about who we really are. It's a chance to discover how much God loves us and believes in us, as he tells us in his Word:

> I call heaven and earth to witness against
> you today, that I have set before you life
> and death, the blessing and the curse. So
> choose life in order that you may live.
> (Deut. 30:19)

THE MIND GAME ...
IT'S NO GAME AT ALL

☙

For as he thinks within himself, so he is.

—PROVERBS 23:7

The phone rang one rainy afternoon. "Hello, Nick, this is Fran Simmons" (not her real name). "I was wondering if you'd consider talking to a friend of mine. Her marriage is in trouble, and it's really killing her."

"Sure, Fran. I'll try to help."

"I know you can help. You helped me so much."

"You're giving me too much credit. We prayed, and God helped. Besides, you did all the hard work. Anyway, tell me what the problem is."

"My friend Beth thinks her husband may be having an affair."

"Does she have proof?"

"No, but he's been very distant and cold to her, and he's out more than he should be."

"Okay, give her my number and tell her to give me a call."

Later Beth did call me, then came in and told me her story. After going through a half box of tissues, she asked, "What should I do?" That's the question counselors never like to hear, because most problems are complex, and few can be solved with one simple answer. Beth and I talked several more times, and I asked her to have her husband, Phil, come in. He agreed, and we had several sessions during which he danced around the real issue. When he finally got comfortable enough, he confessed that he was having an affair with a

> "WHAT SHOULD I DO?" THAT'S THE QUESTION COUNSELORS NEVER LIKE TO HEAR, BECAUSE MOST PROBLEMS ARE COMPLEX, AND FEW CAN BE SOLVED WITH ONE SIMPLE ANSWER.

woman at the hospital where he worked. He explained the situation like this:

> I've never felt this way about anyone. She understands me so well. She likes the same kinds of books I do. We talk for hours, and it never gets boring. She appreciates me so much. Beth just doesn't understand. She's so busy with the kids that she has nothing left for me.

I asked him if we could look more closely at what he'd just told me. He agreed.

"Okay, you say you never felt this way before. What about when you first met Beth?"

"Well, I guess it was sort of the same. We used to laugh and stuff."

"Did she understand you then?"

"Yeah, I guess so. We had plans and dreams. That's why we got married."

"Could you talk to her then?"

"Yeah, we used to go sit by Echo Lake and drink coffee and talk about a lot of things. But she couldn't care less about what interests me now."

"You're sure of that?"

"Yes. All we ever do is fight about the kids, money, the house ... you name it."

Things didn't work out well for Phil and Beth. Why? Because he was playing a mind game. He thought things *should* be different because he *wanted* them to be different. He convinced himself that the excitement of a new relationship was worth more than his wife, his two daughters, his house, and—in many ways—his future. He convinced himself that he deserved more. I pointed out to him that every single problem he had with his wife could very well appear down the line with someone else. He closed his mind to that truth and decided to believe the lie because he wanted what he wanted. Sounds pretty childish from the outside, but to him it was his right, his chance, his opportunity. So he ignored every objection—even the ones he agreed with. Later he left his wife and kids and ended up on a road that I believe leads nowhere.

What's that story got to do with you? Maybe nothing, maybe everything. Phil's problem was that he played a mind game with himself. Even when he realized he might be on the wrong track,

> ◌
>
> ONE OF SATAN'S
> PRIMARY STRATEGIES
> IS TO GET US
> FOCUSED ON THE
> PHYSICAL RATHER
> THAN THE SPIRITUAL.

he rationalized the thought away. He didn't care
about the truth. He wasn't open to any other outcome. You may be like Phil. You may think there's
no way to come through your situation. You may
already have decided it's impossible to survive this
trial. That's a mind game.

God tells us we have an enemy who specializes
in mind games. One of Satan's primary strategies is
to get us focused on the physical rather than the
spiritual: "For the mind set on the flesh is death,
but the mind set on the Spirit is life and peace,
because the mind set on the flesh
is hostile toward God; for it does
not subject itself to the law of God,
for it is not even able to do so, and
those who are in the flesh cannot
please God" (Rom. 8:6–8). We
have to be aware of it and learn
how to fight against it. It's the best
way to avoid delay and maybe
even destruction.

> ❧
>
> THE SINGLE
> WEAPON GOD
> HAS GIVEN TO
> ATTACK THE
> ENEMY IS HIS
> WORD.

Let's take a closer look at the
powerful force that's at war with
us. The Bible tells us its commander is "the father of
lies" (John 8:44). And that's exactly how he works—
by deception. The more lies he can get us to believe,
the weaker we become: "For our struggle is not

against flesh and blood, but against the rulers, against the powers, against the world forces of this darkness, against the spiritual forces of wickedness in the heavenly places. Therefore, take up the full armor of God, so that you will be able to resist in the evil day, and having done everything, to stand firm" (Eph. 6:12–13).

> ℅
>
> IF WE'RE GOING TO SUCCEED AT STARTING OVER, WE NEED TO KNOW WHAT WE'RE UP AGAINST.

Enough books have been written about the armor of God, so I won't explain each piece. But the picture is that of a soldier going into battle fully prepared. Each of the various pieces (the breastplate of righteousness, the shield of faith, etc.) has a specific function in battle. They're all important, but I'd like to draw your attention to two of them—the sword of the Spirit and the helmet of salvation.

Ephesians 6:17 describes the armor's only offensive weapon as the "sword of the Spirit, which is the word of God." The single weapon God has given to attack the enemy is his Word. That's critical because the primary battle takes place in the mind, and the missiles fired back and forth are thoughts. God's Word can overpower *any* thought of *any* kind.

A counselor friend of mine used to like to say his job was helping people get rid of "stinking thinking." That may be a funny way to say it, but it's dead on target. Everything starts with a thought. Some actions are more noticeable, but no action takes place without a thought preceding it. So we must reclaim the ground we have lost (or forfeited) to the enemy. Our mind must be clear and able to help and not hinder our decision-making process—and it must be filled with the ammunition of God's Word.

If all this sounds mysterious—it is! We are physical beings, but we live in a world that's as much spiritual as physical. If we're going to succeed at starting over, we need to know what we're up against.

In 1 Thessalonians 5:8 the apostle Paul describes the helmet of salvation as "a helmet, the hope of salvation." The key word is *hope*—hope in the eventual good outcome that God has promised. Paul continues that passage in verses 9–11: "For God has not destined us for wrath, but for obtaining salvation through our Lord Jesus Christ, who died for us, so that whether we are awake or asleep, we will live together with Him. Therefore encourage one another and build up one another, just as you also are doing."

Hope lives in the mind. If we believe God knows our frustration and pain, that he's a loving Father who will eventually bring us through, if we believe that in the end we will attain a wonderful eternal existence ... then we can put that powerful hope into our arsenal.

God's Word tells us that "faith, hope, love, abide" (1 Cor. 13:13). They're listed as three essentials for survival in this difficult world. Love gives us a taste of the heavenly relationship to which God is calling us. Faith gives us something to hold on to in the battle of life. Hope gives us a reason to fight on, to stand up to our enemy and say, "I will *not* give up."

> IF THE ENEMY CAN GET YOU TO THINK OF YOURSELF IN ANY WAY OTHER THAN THE WAY GOD SEES YOU, YOU'RE ALREADY LOSING GROUND.

Here's how Paul describes the battle in 2 Corinthians 10:3–5: "For though we walk in the flesh, we do not war according to the flesh, for the weapons of our warfare are not of the flesh, but divinely powerful for the destruction of fortresses. We are destroying speculations and every lofty thing raised up against the knowledge of God, and we are taking every thought captive to the obedience of Christ."

Paul tells us plainly that this battle isn't fought on natural terms. It's not about tanks and planes, muscles and stamina. It's about identifying our spiritual enemy and using spiritual weapons that are effective against him. All the willpower in the world is no match for the assault that will come against us. We can't use natural weapons to win a supernatural war.

What does Paul mean by the "destruction of fortresses"? Some translations say "strongholds." A *stronghold* (or *fortress*) is a "place" we have lost or given up. It's a place in our soul where we have allowed the enemy to set up camp.

For example, a young boy feels rejection at an early age. It hurts him deeply, and he doesn't understand it. Then, as a teenager, he experiences more of the same. He begins to think there's something wrong with him. He feels insignificant, inferior, and worthless. Fast-forward to a young lady telling him, after three years, that she no longer wants to see him.

Now he not only allows the thoughts of insignificance, inferiority, and worthlessness to come into his mind and heart—he entertains them, dwells on them. (Jesus said, "Why do you entertain evil thoughts in your hearts?" [Matt. 9:4 NIV].) He doesn't fight them off. At some point, he becomes so comfortable with them, he actually welcomes them in. Pretty soon those thoughts become a major stronghold.

∾

"Destroying speculations ..." When I think of speculations, I think of all the "what if ..." questions: *What if the relationship hadn't ended? What if the business hadn't failed? What if I'd become vice president of the company? What if I'd never had that car accident? What if my parents had treated me better when I was young?* These are all speculations. But Paul goes a step further. He says that we are to destroy not only speculations but also "every lofty thing raised up against the knowledge of God."

Here's how that action fits into your battle plan. If the enemy can get you to think of yourself in any way other than the way God sees you, you're already losing ground. God looks at you as significant, valuable, and worth fighting for. So when contrary thoughts come into your mind, you must recognize them as "speculations" and "lofty things" that will harm you. They are thoughts "raised up" against God and against the truth about you. You must attack and destroy them before they destroy you. Paul says you must "tak[e] every thought captive to the obedience of Christ."

At this point you may be saying, "Great. So how exactly do I do that?" The answer is simple: You use that part of the spiritual armor designed for attack— "the sword of the Spirit, which is the word of God."

God's words are very powerful:

> Then God said, "Let there be light"; and
> there was light. (Gen. 1:3)

> They came to Jesus and woke Him up,
> saying, "Master, Master, we are perish-
> ing!" And He got up and rebuked the
> wind and the surging waves, and they
> stopped, and it became calm. (Luke 8:24)

When we use God's Word, our enemy cannot overpower it—he must obey it.

Take the young man who has developed a stronghold of worthlessness. He is regularly bombarded with negative attacks against his self-concept: *You just can't cut it. You're a loser. Look at your situation—you may as well curl up and die. You don't have any idea what to do next, do you?*

YOUR SOUL AND SPIRIT—AND YOUR ABILITY TO FIND TRUE JOY— ARE AT STAKE.

As long as the young man accepts these lies, he is under their power. But if he fights back, he can overcome them. Here's how it works: When the thoughts come, he learns to identify them. Then he fights back

with the only thing that's more powerful. He quotes
Scripture, out loud if possible, to force the thoughts
away. After awhile, he realizes that God's Word really
does have power. God's Word is true, and it says
something entirely different about him than what he
has believed. The stronghold begins to crumble. The
truth begins to set him free. Here's what might be
happening inside his head:

> Thought: *You just can't cut it.*
> Answer: "I can do all things through
> Christ who strengthens me" (Phil.
> 4:13 NKJV).
> Thought: *You're a loser.*
> Answer: "I am the righteousness of
> God in Christ" (see 2 Cor. 5:21).
> Thought: *Look at your situation—you
> may as well curl up and die.*
> Answer: "The mind set on the flesh is
> death, but the mind set on the
> Spirit is life and peace" (Rom. 8:6).
> Thought: *You don't have any idea what
> to do next, do you?*
> Answer: "Seek first His kingdom and His
> righteousness, and all these things
> will be added to you" (Matt. 6:33).

This is no simple formula. It's not an easy way out—there are none. It is, however, a powerful tool that takes time and energy to master. If you're not familiar with God's Word, you won't be able to call it to mind when you need it. You must commit to the Word and decide that you'll do whatever it takes to have it in your heart and mind so you can use it. You must believe it's worth the effort. Without it, you're defenseless.

People use the expression "mind games" to describe attempts to manipulate another person into accomplishing some selfish goal. Paul isn't talking about mind games. He's talking about an intense war. Your soul and spirit—and your ability to find true joy—are at stake.

During times of change and unrest, you're more vulnerable than at other times. Your enemy knows that fact. Recognize self-defeating thoughts. Understand where they're coming from. Do as Paul says in 1 Timothy 6:12: "Fight the good fight of faith." No one can fight it for you.

The greatest evidence that this is the only way to win the battle for the mind is found in the actual encounter between Satan and Jesus described in Matthew 4:3–11. Satan throws out three destructive thoughts; Jesus answers each one with God's Word:

Satan: "If You are the Son of God, command that these stones become bread."

Jesus: "It is written, 'Man shall not live on bread alone, but on every word that proceeds out of the mouth of God.'"

Satan: "If You are the Son of God, throw Yourself down; for it is written, 'He will command His angels concerning You'; and 'On their hands they will bear You up, so that You will not strike Your foot against a stone.'"

Jesus: "On the other hand, it is written, 'You shall not put the Lord your God to the test.'"

Satan: "All these things I will give You, if You fall down and worship me."

Jesus: "Go, Satan! For it is written, 'You shall worship the Lord your God, and serve Him only.'"

The tactics haven't changed over the centuries. "*If* You are the Son of God ..." If you are struggling with feelings of doubt, fear, and insignificance—remember where those thoughts come from and fight back. That attack takes place in the mind. Some may call it a mind game—but it's no game at all:

> For though we walk in the flesh, we do not war according to the flesh, for the weapons of our warfare are not of the flesh, but divinely powerful for the destruction of fortresses. We are destroying speculations and every lofty thing raised up against the knowledge of God, and we are taking every thought captive to the obedience of Christ. (2 Cor. 10:3–5)

4

CAN A CHRISTIAN BE DEPRESSED?

I lie awake, I have become like a lonely bird on a housetop.

—PSALM 102:7

My first experience with depression occurred when I was about four months into interferon treatment. At first, it was just a sense of overwhelming fatigue. Then, my mood started to decline. Soon afterward, I felt very confused, almost unable to make a decision. I remember being in a video store and getting close to tears because I couldn't decide on a movie.

Concentration became very difficult. I felt very agitated but at the same time physically exhausted. Nothing I did provided any relief. I couldn't distract myself by reading, watching a movie, taking a walk, or anything else. I didn't want to sit still, but I didn't have the energy to go anywhere. Nothing seemed appealing. Every thought added to the exhaustion, and none brought enough motivation to take action.

It was terrifying. For one of the first times in my life, I felt like I was losing control—even more than when I first learned I had a serious illness, even more than when I had to leave my company. In those times, I could use my mind to figure out a way to adapt. But this was different—my mind was the problem.

> ℭ
>
> I KNEW I HAD TO MOVE AND I KNEW I HAD TO PRAY, BUT I COULDN'T EVEN FIGURE OUT HOW TO DO THAT.

Over the next few years, the struggle came and went. At times it was very tough, and at other times it was easier. It took time to understand what was happening to me. It took time and experience to realize I could get through it.

One particularly difficult episode came in midwinter. I was really struggling. I felt helpless and very afraid. I knew I had to move and I knew I had to pray, but I couldn't even figure out how to do that. Finally, I went outside with a shovel in my hand. I thought maybe I could tire myself out and slow down my mind with a bit of physical exercise.

Alone in my driveway, fear drove me to cry out to God. With each shovelful of snow, I said out loud, "The blood of Jesus. The blood of Jesus." I must have said it a hundred

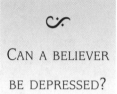

CAN A BELIEVER

BE DEPRESSED?

times. I said it with desperation, but somewhere deep down I knew that he alone could help me. Little by little, my spirit and my heart grew calmer— not immediately and not drastically, but slowly, almost unnoticeably. After awhile, I felt my mind beginning to slow down. I began to feel a spark of hope that control was coming back. Exactly how that worked, I don't know. What I do know is I called on God's power—and I know he heard!

I didn't come back in the house singing and whistling a tune. I came in with a little more peace and a stronger sense that God wouldn't fail me. Over the past few years, I've found ways to work through my depression. I've had some medical help, and I've changed some things in my lifestyle. But by far the most helpful thing has been praying and learning to trust God: learning that God has power over everything; learning to focus on him and his instructions in his Word and by his Spirit. Depression is another challenge we must face in a fallen world. But, as I give myself to God wholeheartedly, he never fails to give me what I need, just as he promised all those who put their faith and trust in him: "He will respond to the prayer of the destitute; he will not despise their plea" (Ps. 102:17 NIV).

න

Can a believer be depressed? Ask Elijah. Ask Job. Ask the apostle Paul. Ask Charles Spurgeon. Ask any of the hundreds of pastors around the country who have battled with the condition. Ask the thousands of believers around the world who have stood up to the assault of darkness and despair. It's real, and it's painful. Can a believer be depressed? The answer is yes.

The psalmist described his depression this way:

Hear my prayer, O Lord! And let my cry
for help come to You. Do not hide Your
face from me in the day of my distress;
incline Your ear to me; in the day when I

call answer me quickly. For my days have
been consumed in smoke, and my bones
have been scorched like a hearth. My
heart has been smitten like grass and has
withered away, indeed, I forget to eat my
bread. Because of the loudness of my
groaning my bones cling to my flesh. I
resemble a pelican of the wilderness; I
have become like an owl of the waste
places. I lie awake, I have become like a
lonely bird on a housetop. (Ps. 102:1–7)

Depression isn't the same thing as a down day or
a sad feeling. It's not boredom. It's a clinical syn-
drome in which the body reacts to physical or
emotional stress, eventually altering the body's
chemistry to the point that mood is affected, energy
is depleted, and the will to live is challenged.

The National Institute of Mental Health says:

A depressive disorder is an illness that
involves the body, mood, and thoughts.
It affects the way a person eats and
sleeps, the way one feels about oneself,
and the way one thinks about things. A
depressive disorder is not the same as a
passing blue mood. It is not a sign of

> personal weakness or a condition that can
> be willed or wished away. People with a
> depressive illness cannot merely "pull
> themselves together" and get better.
> Without treatment, symptoms can last for
> weeks, months, or years. Appropriate
> treatment, however, can help most
> people who suffer from depression.[1]

Not everyone who goes through a dramatic change suffers from clinical depression. Some people encounter a life-changing situation, start all over, and make it through the transition without any negative consequences at all. You may be one of those who have gone though such experiences without having to deal with the added burden of chronic depression. If so, please be sensitive to those who aren't as fortunate as you are.

> **GOD AND HIS WORD ARE THE BEST ANTI-DEPRESSANTS EVER CREATED.**

Whatever you do, don't tell others who are truly depressed, "Keep your chin up." Don't tell them just to *refuse* to be depressed. Don't look at them like they're weak or lack willpower. Don't be like Job's friends and tell them there must be sin in their lives. Sin usually isn't the issue for depressed believers. That's because when they feel threatened, one of the first things they usually do is ask God's forgiveness and beg for mercy. So, in my opinion, it's rare for sin to be the cause of *true* believers' depressions. It may be a different story for nonbelievers or those who profess to believe but who haven't truly accepted Christ's lordship in their lives.

> ᘓ
>
> THOSE WHO LIVE WITHOUT FAITH MUST DEPEND ON THEIR OWN RESOURCES, WHILE THOSE WHO LIVE BY FAITH CAN CALL ON ALMIGHTY GOD FOR HELP.

So what do you do if (a) you are a believer, and (b) you are depressed?

First, recognize that God doesn't condemn you. Jesus said, "Come to Me, all who are weary and heavy-laden, and I will give you rest" (Matt. 11:28). Not every person who is weary or heavy-laden is depressed, but every person who is depressed is both weary and heavy-laden. Jesus welcomes that person into his arms with understanding and compassion. Dismiss the thought that God doesn't accept you because of your pain. On the contrary—the psalmist wrote in Psalm 34:18, "The Lord is near to the brokenhearted and saves those who are crushed in spirit."

Next, realize that nothing will help you as much as God and his Word. His Word must never be far from your mind. Why? Because it is the best antidepressant ever created. It is the single most powerful antidote to any and every negative thought. (I'm not a doctor, and I don't pretend to be one. In some cases medication is needed, and I don't see taking it as weakness at all. I believe God can work with anyone to overcome the cause of depression, but it may take time. Find a good doctor—preferably one who believes what you do about God.) Take direction from a medical professional, but put it all under God's supervision. In Psalm 32:8 God himself says, "I will instruct you and teach you in the way which you should go." You can count on it.

> CHRISTIANS CAN BE DEPRESSED, BUT CHRISTIANS SHOULD NEVER BE HOPELESS.

A doctor can advise you about diet and exercise—and those things do make a difference. But, in my opinion, nothing comes close to the help God can and will give you if you genuinely seek him.

There's one main difference between living a life of faith and living a life without faith. It's not that those who live without faith invite troubles, while those who live by faith skate through life unscathed. It's not that one group enjoys moments of happiness while the other never does. If that is so, what is the difference? It's the fact that those who live without faith must depend on their own resources, while those who live by faith can call on almighty God for help.

Anytime you're forced to start over, you're given an opportunity to assess things anew: *How do I make decisions? How do I handle adversity? Where do I go when I need help? Whom can I count on when life lets me down?* The answers to all these questions are the same, and the God who made you knows what those answers are. If you're trying to make it through life without him and his knowledge and wisdom, you may not be fighting through a cloud of depression— but you're fighting just the same.

In John 16:33, the Lord told his disciples, "In the world you have tribulation, but take courage; I have overcome the world." That statement applies to everyone.

Peter warned the believers of his day, "Beloved, do not be surprised at the fiery ordeal among you, which comes upon you for your testing, as though some strange thing were happening to you" (1 Peter 4:12).

That warning also applies to us today. It's the human condition to be challenged by difficulties. Those who are wise prepare before the difficulties come.

Christians can be depressed, but Christians should never be hopeless. Again and again, we see in the Bible that those who had faith and hope in God's provision suffered less depression and came through it with greater ease than those who did not have that faith and hope.

Read David's cry to the Lord recorded in Psalm 13:1–6. Notice how he worked himself through to a place of confidence in God, even though his confidence was severely weakened:

> How long, O Lord? Will You forget me forever? How long will You hide Your face from me? How long shall I take counsel in my soul, having sorrow in my heart all the day? How long will my enemy be exalted over me? Consider and answer me, O Lord my God; enlighten my eyes, or I will sleep the sleep of death, and my enemy will say, "I have overcome him," and my adversaries will rejoice when I am shaken. But I have trusted in Your lovingkindness; my heart shall rejoice in Your salvation. I will sing

to the Lord, because He has dealt boun-
tifully with me.

Look at Elijah, Job, Jeremiah, and Paul. They
were all great men of God, but it appears they all
battled some degree of depression. They all came
through stronger and more aware of their need for
God.

There is a gift born out of this misery. Learning
to depend on God in such a desperate way is a lesson that will bear fruit the rest of our life. I know.
I've traveled the dark and despairing road myself—
but take heart. Guess who I found there? Yes, and
amen! The Light of the World traveled with me.
Paul summed up this wonderful life of faith in these
words:

> More than that, I count all things to be
> loss in view of the surpassing value of
> knowing Christ Jesus my Lord, for whom
> I have suffered the loss of all things, and
> count them but rubbish so that I may
> gain Christ, and may be found in Him,
> not having a righteousness of my own
> derived from the Law, but that which is
> through faith in Christ, the righteousness
> which comes from God on the basis of

faith, that I may know Him and the power of His resurrection and the fellowship of His sufferings, being conformed to His death; in order that I may attain to the resurrection from the dead. (Phil. 3:8–11)

"I Never Thought of It That Way!"

Oh my soul, be prepared for the coming
of the Stranger. Be prepared for him who
knows how to ask questions.

—T. S. ELIOT

A plane droned monotonously overhead. A bird
chirped lazily. Cars hummed by on the street in front
of my house while I sat choking on reality. I realized
I was no longer part of the onrushing current of
everyday life. I had nothing to do and nowhere to
go. The feeling of uselessness was overwhelming.

What am I supposed to do now? I asked myself. I had tried a lot of different things to fill the time, but none of them satisfied for long. I thought I could keep God in the background as a fail-safe. I "hunkered down" and tried to make sense of my new reality. Everything I tried fell flat. I was left discouraged and close to hopeless.

That's when I realized I was still looking for *my* way out. I was trying to redefine myself. I was trying to meet God on my terms. I should have been asking him who I really was, instead of trying to create something new on my own. In the end, no matter how hard I tried other ways—it always came back to trusting him.

> IF YOU'RE LOOKING FOR GOD'S HELP, START BY UNLOADING ALL YOUR CONDITIONS.

One day I just stopped asking myself, *Who am I now?* It suddenly made more sense to ask him that question. After all, he's the Communicator of whole truth—and that means more than just the part that suits me.

If you're looking for God's help, start by unloading all your conditions. They do nothing but get in the way. It isn't, "I'll come to you if you do this for me," or, "This is who I think I should be. Would you please make it happen?" It's, "I'll come to you because I've come to the end of myself, and I need you." It's responding without conditions to his invitation: "Take My yoke upon you and learn from Me, for I am gentle and humble in heart, and you will find rest for your souls" (Matt. 11:29).

When it started, I had no idea why the question about my identity kept coming up. I thought it might have been a self-defeating mood or an emotional reaction to sudden change. I thought it might be the evil questioner who provokes confusion. But I've come to believe it was none of those. I believe it was almighty God inviting me to begin a crucial journey—a journey to true understanding of my purpose and value. David O. McKay said, "The most important of life's battles is the one we fight daily in the silent chambers of the soul."[1]

You may be in that position right now. If you are, here are a few thoughts that may help you make an accurate assessment of yourself and your situation.

1. Ask yourself what really matters in the big picture of your life. What drives you to go on? Do you have a family that cares about you? That's a good place to start. Suspend your discouragement for a minute and consider the people who love you. If you're

fortunate enough to have that kind of love in your life, you're already miles ahead of many people.

Think about what you've been through with those closest to you. Is their love for you conditional? What do they want most for you? You may think they want you to be X, Y, or Z, but the truth is they don't care that much about what you do or your life circumstance. They care about you and want you to be happy. How do you treat them? How much love and support do you show them? Are you available when they need you? Start with an honest evaluation of those closest to you. Almost always, you'll find that you care more about what you are and what you do than they do.

2. Ask yourself what you think life is all about. In other words, why are you here and where are you going? If you can honestly say you're God-created, you have the answer to the question of your value well within your grasp. Here's why: If in fact God made you, he had a purpose and a plan. He made you valuable to him. You don't have to find things that make you valuable. He already has bestowed that value on you. We'll explore this subject in greater depth later,

but for now, just think about this: God has
never lost interest in you. He has never lost
the desire to guide you and bless you. Accept
life for what it is—a journey of discovery.
You'll only find accurate directions in relationship with the One who knows the way.

3. Ask yourself who really knows the truth
about life. Is it the corporate executives who
live by the bottom line? Is it the editorialists
and pundits who spout self-assured opinions?
Is it the successful people, who own and control more than most and suffer the highest
degree of mental and emotional illness? No.

If you want the truth, you have to go to
the Truth. Jesus Christ is "the way, and the
truth, and the life" (John 14:6). He never
once said anything that wasn't entirely true.
Numbers 23:19 indicates who can always be
trusted: "God is not a man, that He should
lie, nor a son of man, that He should repent;
has He said, and will He not do it? Or has
He spoken, and will He not make it good?"

I believe the answers to these three questions will
be immensely helpful and will give you a solid foundation on which to build a new life based on a new
perspective of yourself. Opening yourself to the truth
always weakens the grip of confusion and heartbreak.

Robert McGee, in his book *The Search for Significance*, wrote: "When the light of love and honesty shines on thoughts of hopelessness, it's often very painful. We begin to admit that we really do feel negatively about ourselves—and have for a long time. But God's love, expressed through his people and woven into our lives by his Spirit and his Word, can, over a period of time, bring healing even to our deepest wounds and instill within us an appropriate sense of self-worth."[2]

> ℃
>
> IF YOU CAN HONESTLY SAY YOU'RE GOD-CREATED, YOU HAVE THE ANSWER TO THE QUESTION OF YOUR VALUE WELL WITHIN YOUR GRASP.

He also wrote: "Ask the Lord to give you the courage to be honest. Give him permission to shine his Spirit's light on your thoughts, feelings, and actions. Some additional pain may surprise you as you realize the extent of your wounds, but our experience of healing can only be as deep as our awareness of the need for it."[3]

If your seeking is genuine, you will meet God. If you really want to know who you are—with or without your work, your spouse, or your status or position—only God can show you. Don't give up. God knows the way, and he not only can help you, he wants to help you. One of the first things he may teach you to say is, "I never thought of it that way!"

I can do all things through Him who strengthens me. (Phil. 4:13)

6

"Who, Exactly, Does God Say I Am?"

> I said, "You are gods, and all of you are
> children of the Most High."
>
> —Psalm 82:6 NKJV

I had been home on disability for close to a year
when Dawn and I decided to condense some of our
bank accounts. One morning, I drove to my neighborhood bank. I walked in and went to one of the
service desks.

"Hi, can I help you?" the assistant manager asked.

"I'd like to close out two older accounts we have
with the bank and open a new checking account," I
said with a smile.

"Sure, that will be fine. Have a seat, and I'll pull out the paperwork." She was very pleasant and professional. We chatted about the weather and family. I commented on her daughter's picture, which sat prominently on her desk.

"Okay, Mr. Gugliotti. Start with this form for opening the new account, and then we'll see about closing the accounts you don't need anymore."

Name, address, Social Security number, number of years at this residence ... everything was going along smoothly until I reached the line that read *Occupation.* I swallowed and stared at the word as though I couldn't understand what it meant. I knew I no longer had an occupation; I knew the correct answer was "disabled." But I'd just talked about my family and how proud I was of my two children. I'd done my best to exude an air of competence and command. Now, I was supposed to write down "disabled." It felt like I was putting a sticker on my forehead that read "incompetent" or "useless."

> I KNEW I NO LONGER HAD AN OCCUPATION; I KNEW THE CORRECT ANSWER WAS "DISABLED."

"Everything okay, Mr. Gugliotti? Is there anything you need help with?" she asked.

"Oh no, everything is fine," I said.

Eventually I finished opening the new account and closing the two old ones. I said good-bye and left the bank. Sitting in my car, I felt uncomfortable. I'd written down "writer" instead of "disabled" because I was embarrassed to say I was disabled due to illness. I'd fumbled through the conversation when the assistant manager asked me

> ᴄ⁀
>
> I SIMPLY JUDGED MYSELF, DISMISSED MYSELF, AND LABELED MYSELF A LOSER BECAUSE I DIDN'T FEEL THAT I MEASURED UP TO SOME SELF-IMPOSED STANDARD.

about what I wrote. Although it's true I've always written, I knew I'd answered with a deliberate half truth. I felt dishonest.

And that's where a great danger lies. If I'd told the truth and explained what my situation was, the woman might have been sympathetic or she might not have cared. But I removed the possibility of a good outcome. I simply judged myself, dismissed myself, and labeled myself a loser because I didn't feel that I measured up to some self-imposed standard.

I remember asking God to forgive me for judging myself so harshly. I asked him to forgive me for falling into the trap of caring about what others "might" think, rather than caring about what he thinks. It was an important lesson for me.

Don't make the mistake I made. If you think people look at you a certain way because you're single or divorced or out of work; if you, for whatever reason, feel judged ... come to terms with the situation. Consider these points: (1) If people form an opinion of you without knowledge of you or your situation, their opinion is less than meaningful, and (2) if you form the wrong opinion of yourself, you lock yourself in a prison of self-doubt from which it is very hard to escape. Don't do it. Ask God to help you see yourself as you *really* are.

> ❧
>
> I RESENT IT WHEN PEOPLE THINK THEY KNOW ME JUST BY ASKING A FEW SUPERFICIAL QUESTIONS ABOUT WHAT I DO FOR A LIVING.

❧

Maybe you don't have a title or a nine-to-five job. Or maybe you've finished parenting or your spouse has died or left. It could be that you're no longer needed the way you once were. If so, that doesn't make you a "nobody."

Unfortunately, some people do make judgments about us based on our circumstances. Sometimes it's subconscious; sometimes it's just the easy way out. I resent it when people think they know me just by asking a few superficial questions about what I do for a living. But to be honest, I slip into making wrong judgments of myself—and others—if I don't make a conscious effort not to do so. As human beings we all pigeonhole one another. It's not fair, but it happens all the time. Being falsely judged is never enjoyable, but we can diffuse its power if we realize how inaccurate and invalid it usually is.

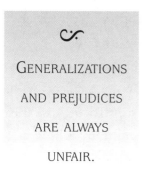

GENERALIZATIONS AND PREJUDICES ARE ALWAYS UNFAIR.

Often, when people want to know who a person is, they ask for name and occupation. They ask about marriage, children, neighborhood, and so on. Dr. Chris Thurman, psychologist with the Minirth-Meier Clinic, offers a better standard of understanding our true identity: "I believe self-esteem comes from who made us, not what we do. We need to view ourselves in 'vertical' dimensions—seeing who we are in God's eyes, not the 'horizontal' dimensions of doing all we can to impress others through achievement or success. God sees us as having great worth because he created us in his image. Now that is a true basis for self-esteem."[1]

People often use shortcuts or stereotypes to label others. It's easier to be superficial. But ask a young mother who has decided to stay home and raise her children how she feels when an arrogant career woman speaks to her in a condescending tone, referring to her as "just a housewife." Or ask the older gentleman how he feels when someone implies he has nothing to do now that he's "retired from the workforce." And what about the divorced man who feels judged by those who are happily married before they know anything about him or his circumstances, or the young lady who is made to feel inadequate or undesirable because she has never found the right man and maybe never will?

Maybe you feel unfairly judged because of your circumstances. If so, you have two choices: (1) You can become bitter about it, or (2) you can accept the fact that people's superficial judgments are often wrong and in reality carry no weight.

Generalizations and prejudices are always unfair. They can be based on skin color, gender, age, style of worship, level of income, or marital status—almost anything that adds up to *opinion without knowledge.*

Would you like to see how easy it is to judge incorrectly? Try this little experiment. I'll name a profession; you focus on your first impression. Don't try to make yourself a "good" person by editing your thoughts. Stay on each one for about ten or fifteen seconds. Write the first words that come to mind.

Doctor

Senator

Garbage collector

Odd-job specialist

Priest

Most people probably think highly of the doctor. They assume that person is educated and competent, dedicated and successful. Some would think less of the garbage collector and the odd-job specialist because they have no "position" in life. And some would respect the senator or the priest based on the title, while others would prejudge them due to negative things they've heard about senators or priests.

In every case, the perceptions are nothing more than stereotypes.

Take, for example, the following profiles based on actual people I know.

The doctor is a highly respected practitioner, regarded by many as one of the best in his field. However, he's a very unsuccessful human being. His two marriages ended in divorce. He doesn't see his children. He drinks to forget his pain. He dislikes his profession and his patients. And he has contemplated suicide more than once.

The senator is a well-adjusted family man. He's never compromised his values for selfish gain. He represents his constituents with honesty and compassion. He cares deeply about his friends and family. Though he's well educated, he gravitates toward relationships with people who aren't part of the "in-crowd."

The garbage collector grew up in a good family but never excelled in school. After many frustrations and disappointments, he decided to stop trying to be something he couldn't be. He resolved to be content and make the best of his life. He never misses work and does his job with joy. His coworkers, even the cynical ones, like him. He volunteers at the soup kitchen in town and gives what he can to charity. He lives a peaceful life surrounded by a loving family.

The man who does odd jobs is a hardworking immigrant. He came from poverty, yet never ceases to thank God for all he has. He has no career per se. He helped start a church and often spends twelve to fifteen hours working by day and ministering by night. His face shines with God's love. His car is old, and his house is basic, yet he greets each day with excitement and a clear sense of purpose.

The priest is a genuine man of God. He is an advocate for peace and an unselfish servant of those in need. Those who would blindly categorize him would miss the humble integrity of his life and the Christlike compassion that defines him.

Based on this description of each of these people, has your stereotypical perception of any of them based on their titles been affected by specific factual information about each of them?

In the same way that you may have unfairly judged each of these people, so others will often judge you unfairly; but you don't have to do that to yourself. To base your estimation of yourself on the opinion of others is to make yourself a target. You can learn to take others' opinion of you for what it's worth—nothing. You are a God-made being. As such, only God can show you the essence of who you are. If you look anywhere else for your identity and sense of self-worth, you are bound to be disappointed.

I was shocked to read a story that demonstrates just how far this sense of insecurity can go. A premed honor student and track star was invited to compete in the NCAA nationals. She was a very good distance runner and entered the race as one of the favorites, considering it a stepping-stone to bigger and better things. In the championship race, she ran well but finished second. When the race ended, she kept on running. She ran out of the arena,

straight to a nearby bridge, and jumped off. As a
result of that rash, thoughtless act, that young lady
is now permanently paralyzed from the waist down.

In a weak moment,
she confused her personal
worth with her personal
performance. She thought
she couldn't live with losing. She didn't leave room
for another day or another
race. She didn't consider
another outcome. The
results were devastating.

> ∽
>
> GOD KNOWS OUR
> MOST IMPORTANT NEXT
> STEP IN LIFE—OUR JOB
> IS TO ASK HIM TO HELP
> US FIND IT!

Who we are is not
based on circumstances or performance.

Our children are valuable because of who they
are—not because of what they do or the circumstances of their lives. The same is true of us as God's
children.

A young man left a lucrative job to work with
troubled teens. He imagined that the right kind of
work would help him find a sense of true significance. Here's what he learned after two years on
the job:

> The only thing tougher than that first
> year of living with juvenile delinquents

was the second year. By its end, I felt burned out, used up, spiritually dry, profoundly disappointed, and very angry. I'd left my successful career to work with a handful of troubled teens, and they didn't seem to be getting any better. In fact, it looked more like they were getting worse.

All I had wanted was to make a difference—for my life to have lasting significance. Had I missed God's calling? And where was all this anger coming from? It got so bad that at one point I couldn't even attend our evening devotions, because of anger and hatred I was harboring toward one of the boys living with us ...

I began meeting with an older accountability partner, trying to understand what God was saying in all of this. In the process, I came to realize my dominant need was to make a lasting, significant difference. That's why I left a successful career as a stockbroker to go to seminary. It's why I believed that opening a home for juvenile offenders was a worthwhile sacrifice.

While that's a noble desire, I had a faulty understanding of where my ultimate

sense of significance comes from. It can
only be found in Jesus Christ. Graciously,
God grants us significant and worthwhile
things to do in this life, but our deepest
needs for significance will never be met in
those things. Only he can meet that need.[2]

God knows our most important next step in life—
our job is to ask him to help us find it! When we do,
other people's judgments won't matter. God alone
knows our true identity. In order to discover it, we
must come face-to-face with him. Seeing ourselves
reflected in his eyes is the beginning of understanding who we truly are. Seeing God reflected in our
eyes is the beginning of other people's realization.

I had a hard time with that concept. My family
was made up largely of hardworking immigrants who
were concerned about their reputation. They wanted
to be seen as good citizens with admirable values and
loving families. Consequently, we were taught to be
very aware of our attitudes and behavior. I remember
my father being most proud of us when others
noticed how well we were doing.

With that upbringing, I had an ingrained need for
outside acceptance. Looking back, I know good
intentions led to that thinking. But the fact is, it can be
crippling. I've come to learn that if I can stand before

God honestly, with all my faults, and still be accepted by him, everything and everyone else's opinion must stand aside. The only fair and trustworthy assessment of who I am comes from the One who made me.

Our true identity doesn't come from accomplishments, status, or circumstances. It's inherent within us because God put it there. In his book *My Utmost for His Highest*, Oswald Chambers put it this way: "By regeneration the Son of God is formed in us, and in our physical life he has the same setting that he had on earth. Satan doesn't tempt us to do wrong things, he tempts us in order to make us lose what God has put into us by regeneration— the possibility of being of value to God."[3]

Put simply, we are undone when we believe we are unworthy of Christ's death on the cross. Faith opens a door to experiencing God's complete acceptance and approval. Satan says, "You *are not* worthy." God says, "You *are* worthy." Satan says, "You are *orphaned*." God says, "I *have adopted you as my own*."

> LOOKING TO THE WORLD TO DISCOVER OUR IDENTITY IS LIKE LOOKING AT A FUN-HOUSE MIRROR —FROM ANY ANGLE, IT'S ALWAYS DISTORTED.

Looking to the world to discover our identity is like looking at a fun-house mirror—from any angle, it's always distorted. Looking to God to discover our true self allows us to see the whole truth. We are not valuable because others say so, but because God has made it so—and that's the true significance of self-discovery.

∽

Al Elsdon, a "retired" pastor and good friend, tells about volunteering to help bring internationally known evangelist Luis Palau to his community. In the planning stages, he received a call from an eager, young campaign associate.

"Hello, Mr. Elsdon, I'm putting together a directory of all the people working on this event. What should I put for a title for you?" Al thought for a while and then said, "Well, I have no title. I'm retired, and I have no job. I guess the truth is I'm 'nobody.'"

In fact, he was playing with words. He knows he is someone in God's eyes and in the eyes of the people he visits in hospitals and homes; in the eyes of the young men who come to him for guidance and counsel; and in the eyes of a family that deeply loves and appreciates him. But he has no official title. He simply does the work God gives him to do each day.

For a long time after my father died, my mother was uncomfortable and unable to fit in. She often called herself a "fifth wheel," which to her meant unnecessary. Not until she became comfortable with her new role in the lives of family and friends did she realize that, although her circumstances had changed, she was still the same person we all greatly loved and deeply valued.

NO MATTER WHO YOU ARE, WHAT YOU DO WITH YOUR TIME, OR WHAT YOU'RE GOING THROUGH, YOU STILL HAVE WORTH AND YOU ARE STILL VALUABLE TO THOSE AROUND YOU.

But you are a chosen race, a royal priesthood, a holy nation, a people for God's own possession, so that you may proclaim the excellencies of Him who has called you out of darkness into His marvelous light; for you once were not a people, but now you are the people of God; you had not received mercy, but

now you have received mercy.
(1 Peter 2:9–10)

Shakespeare wrote, "All the world's a stage, and all the men and women merely players."[4] It's a sad epitaph that reads, "Here lies a man who learned to play his roles well." I didn't realize it, but that could have described me before things changed. Work gave me my persona, my identity—my sense of value. I didn't realize I was operating under such a narrow point of view. I never imagined I'd be so lost when I could no longer do the things I'd done before. And I didn't realize I was about to learn one of the most important lessons of my life: *What we do is not who we are.*

Sometimes it takes a dramatic turn of events to force us to dig deeper. For me, it took the doctor telling me that I had a potentially terminal illness and that I could no longer define myself by my career. Strange as it may sound, I was as troubled about losing my place in this world as I was about leaving this world. I didn't know that work and worth were so closely tied together in my mind. When it became clear I'd be "out of work," I was forced to subtract it from the equation and see what was left. I was shocked by what I discovered.

You may be encountering different life-altering circumstances, but you may be making the same mistake I made. I thought who I was depended on the things I did, the way people looked at me, the way I thought about myself. I found that idea to be one of the biggest deceptions I've ever fallen for.

If you want to get to the core of who you are, you'll have to separate yourself from what you do and even from the people who make up your experience of life. It makes no difference how you spent your time and energy before. What matters is how much you have allowed it to define you.

The scales can easily tip in favor of busyness over faith, family, and future. The great danger is letting what you do become who you are. Jobs change, families grow up, youth turns to old age, and everything changes with time. If you tie yourself too closely to what you once did, you'll bankrupt today and leave yourself vulnerable tomorrow. Jesus taught his disciples to work for "fruit [that] would remain" (John 15:16). Have you ever wondered what you'll remember about your life when it's time for you to die? For me, illness was my wake-up call. The cause of the wake-up call is really not important. It's the response to the alarm that matters.

God declares that it's always good to love him and to love our families, friends, and neighbors. That's the message Christ came to embody. That's what life is all about. The message of this book is this:

No matter who you are, what you do with your time, or what you're going through, you still have worth and you are still valuable to those around you.

You'll first discover that worth and value in a relationship with God. He'll teach you to share what you learn with those he has placed in your life. He can make you a representative of hope in a hopeless world. Once that happens, you'll find

> ℘
>
> DONNA HAD THE
> UNIQUE COMBINATION
> OF WARMTH AND
> INTELLIGENCE.

strength for what lies ahead. This approach doesn't make light of your pain, but it offers you something powerful to hang on to and gives you reason to move forward.

But I'm getting ahead of myself. I still haven't told you about the difficult task of leaving an enterprise I cared deeply about. I had to separate myself from the life I had lived before things changed. I had to say good-bye to the past and understand I couldn't go back. You also may have to come to terms with letting go and not looking back.

℘

I arrived at my office at 6:15 a.m. carrying a bag of bagels. I was usually the first one to get there, and every Friday for years I had always laid out a spread of fresh bagels and cream cheese. I did it because I liked the people I worked with. It was a small way to say, "I appreciate you guys. You're more than colleagues; you're people I care about."

I walked around the office turning on lights and equipment. Everything about the place felt comfortable. It was our place, but in many ways it was my place. I'd put my stamp on it. During the formative years, I'd nurtured it like a baby. Now it was maturing, and I was no longer the only one with a vision. I welcomed the shared vision as a sign of a maturing business, but I never imagined I wouldn't be part of shaping the company's future.

That particular day I didn't come in to help secure the future—I came in to start the process of stepping aside. As I'd done every morning, I sat alone at my desk with my Bible open. I asked God to give me the courage I needed and help me do what I knew had to be done. The

> WE'D WALKED DOWN A COMMON PATH FOR A LONG TIME; THEY WOULD CONTINUE THAT WAY—I WOULD NOT.

conference table at which I'd chaired many meetings stared back at me. The empty chairs reflected my feelings. Framed pieces of our best work hung on the walls, each a reminder of a different time in the process of developing the company, from a one-man consulting service to a well-respected, full-service marketing firm.

Fortunately, disability insurance would provide for my family while I was out on leave. I also knew that Social Security and our prearranged buyout would supplement our income if it turned out I couldn't return. It was a step backward financially, but it was a tremendous blessing to have an income at all. No, money wasn't in the forefront of my mind; saying good-bye to a way of life was.

A few hours later, the office was humming. I buzzed each of my partners and asked them to join me in my office. Donna came in and immediately sensed my somber mood. "What's up?" she asked.

"I need to talk to you guys," I said.

Tom entered the room a few minutes later.

"Close the door, Tom," I said.

When I turned to face them, they read a good bit of the story in the expression on my face.

My personal attachment to my partners made it hard to break away. Our relationship had been fully reciprocal. I had taught them what I knew, and they had taught me things I didn't know. Tom had started out a good person and had eventually become one of the finest creative people I've ever worked with. At first, I felt like a mentor to him. Later, I came to respect his talent and his very fine mind. I always admired the genuinely kind heart that was sometimes invisible to others who were intimidated by his intense personality. Tom helped me learn that people aren't projects. They're not there for us to try to change. He frustrated me at times, and I'm sure I did the same to him. But in the end, I knew we were friends; we respected each other, and we had pooled our energies to build a business that to this day supports many individuals and families. We did it with honesty and hard work—and that's no small accomplishment.

Donna had taught me why it's right to respect the individual regardless of gender. She overcame prejudice with grace. When clients or coworkers underestimated her, she was willing to bide her time. She didn't gain respect through confrontation but through ability. She had the unique combination of warmth and intelligence. She offered a measured sense of control when others panicked. Our ties bound us to our beginnings and a closely held family history. In the end, she may turn out to be the strongest of the original partners.

We were much more than business partners. We prayed together before management meetings. We asked God's blessing and wisdom in our decisions, and I felt I was something of a spiritual counselor to both of them. It made our relationship especially meaningful on many levels. I was blessed to have them in my life. My heart ached as I thought about a future without daily interaction with them.

I gathered my thoughts and sat down at the conference table. They had respectfully remained silent.

Thirty minutes later I'd laid the story out for them. They understood my anguish. We knew the road was now diverging. They were going one way, and I had to go another. We'd walked down a common path for a long time; they would continue that way—I would not.

That night, after everyone had left, I walked around the office looking at individual work areas. Each person represented something to me. I'd spent a tremendous amount of time with these people. We'd been to the hospital to greet each other's babies and at each other's sides when loved ones were buried. We'd been to weddings and picnics. We'd worked together on campaigns and deadlines. For many years, our lives had intersected daily. Soon, that would be just memory. Standing at the back door, I looked back one last time.

Maybe you know the emotional pain that goes with saying good-bye to a way of life. Maybe you've lost an important job or career. Maybe you're struggling with life after a painful divorce. Maybe your plans for the future just fell apart. Maybe your last child just moved away. Maybe a sudden accident has changed everything. Maybe you're struggling with illness.

Whatever it is, I have something I feel very strongly about to say to you. I've experienced it first-hand. My confidence is in the power behind what I've observed, not in my ability to observe it. I would never have seen it without God's help.

Change is often painful, but it's always an invitation to deeper understanding:

> No longer do I call you slaves, for the slave does not know what his master is doing; but I have called you friends, for all things that I have heard from My Father I have made known to you. (Jesus to his disciples in John 15:15)

WHAT WILL YOU SEE IN THE REARVIEW MIRROR?

The only thing you take with you when
you're gone is what you leave behind.

—JOHN ALLSTON

My father was six years old before he met his
father because my grandfather had left a pregnant
wife to cross the Atlantic and come to America. For
several years my grandfather traveled back and forth,
working hard to establish a future for his family. For
months at a time, he lived alone many miles away
from his family. From a very early age, my father

learned that a man must work in order to provide his family a better life.

At sixteen, my father also immigrated to this country. He mastered the language and spoke excellent English. He defended this country as a non-commissioned officer in the U.S. Army. Back in civilian life, he rose up through the ranks from apprentice to master plumber, supervising large projects for a regional plumbing contractor. His quick mind and confident manner gained him the admiration of family and friends alike. I can't remember a time when he worked fewer than two jobs. I can't remember when people wouldn't have classified him as "hardworking." That situation never changed until Dad got sick.

> ᘖ
>
> HE SMILED AT ME WITH GOOD INTENTIONS, BUT HIS FACE BETRAYED THE PAIN OF DIMINISHED CAPACITY.

When he was diagnosed with cancer, he approached it like everything else in his life. He put forth a great effort to fight the disease. When he could no longer work, he had to battle the self-doubt and insecurity of redefining himself without work. It was painful to watch. He pushed himself to be useful.

I remember when my wife and I had just moved into our first house. He came over to panel our basement. He was so tired from chemotherapy and advancing disease that he literally had to sit down every ten minutes or so. I remember coming home from work one day, and there was Dad sitting on an upside-down white bucket. He wanted to get up when I came in, but he just didn't have the energy. This was the man who had always represented strength and stability to me and never seemed overwhelmed by anything. He smiled at me with good intentions, but his face betrayed the pain of diminished capacity. It touched me deeply that he would work slowly and with great difficulty to help me. I learned something very important about his heart that day.

When it finally became apparent he wouldn't win the battle, he put what energy he had left into setting things in order. Ironically, that last phase of his life, when he became the most vulnerable, produced some of the most meaningful memories for me. He didn't need to be in charge or pretend to be strong. All that was left was an honest and loving man. In that state, he was very special to all of us.

I remember all the work he did, but none of it stays in my mind as vividly as the time he gathered us together and made a simple, "final" request. He didn't mention work or houses or possessions. He didn't say a single word about wills or money. He simply said, "Please love each other, and please always stay together." I love him very much for those words. They're valuable words to live by. The measure of his life is contained more in those nine words than in all the great things he accomplished.

In the last months of my father's life, I had the most wonderful conversations with him. I was able to tell him how much he meant to me and how I appreciated all he'd done for my sister, my brother, my mom, and me. He'd lost his sense of indestructibility. He'd become vulnerable and open to me in a way that was much deeper than anything we had previously experienced. I always knew I needed him, but in those last times he let me know he needed me—and that shared dependence bound us together in a way I find hard to describe.

> ℘
>
> HE VALIDATED ME AS A MAN WHEN HE SPOKE TO ME AS SOMEONE HE TRUSTED.

In the end, what I value most isn't that he sent me to college or that we had a nice home and that our bills were paid. I value that he allowed me to share the difficult realities of life with him. I am forever indebted to him, not for all the work—although it was helpful to me—but for the lessons I learned as I watched him in the final stages of his life. I'm indebted to him because when he was weak, he let me be strong. He validated me as a man when he spoke to me as someone he trusted. Now that I'm in a similar position, I carry it in my heart that he walked this road before me. He gave me an example of love, caring, dignity, and integrity. That's an incredible gift for a father to give to a son. I pray every day I'll be able to give it to my son and daughter.

∽

In *A Love Worth Giving*, Max Lucado says, "Think of it this way. When you're in the final days of your life, what will you want? When death extends its hands to you, where will you turn for comfort? Will you hug that college degree in the walnut frame? Will you ask to be carried to the garage so you can sit in your car? Will you find comfort in rereading your financial statement? Of course not. What will matter most then will be people. If relationships will matter most then, shouldn't they matter most now?"[1]

For many years, I thought loving my family meant giving them things. I was sincerely dedicated to work as the vehicle through which I could demonstrate my love and commitment to them. *I thought it was my job.* I told myself, *I am doing this because I love them so much.* Over time, it became an ingrained standard to live by: "love my family—work hard; work hard—love my family." I couldn't see it any other way.

Then circumstances forced me to reconsider. Providing for my family's material needs is certainly a good thing, but it's not the best thing. Understanding the broader scope of what my family needs is much more important. They need me to work at a loving and respectful relationship with them. They need me to spend time with them. They need me to have patience so I don't jump down their throats, correcting them at every turn. They need to look up and see me there and know I'm not in a rush to leave. They need me to spend time knowing God so I can help them know God. They need to see me living unselfishly so they can learn to be unselfish. These are the priorities I now hang on to.

> ☙
>
> THE PERSON WHO HAS RETIRED STILL HAS THIS IMPORTANT WORK TO DO, AS DOES THE MAN WHO HAS BECOME ILL AND THE WOMAN WHO HAS LOST THE LOVE OF HER LIFE.

When I consider what really lasts, the facts clearly point to matters of the heart. In my mind's eye, I see my eight-year-old son beaming after making a game-saving catch to end a Little League ball game. He and I walk up to the ice cream truck, and the man inside says, "This kid's ice cream is free after that catch." My son looks at me, and I look at him; without a word we experience the joy of that shared moment. That connection is priceless.

I see my daughter at a high school track meet. I stand behind the fence; she stands just past the finish line. She has just won her first race, and the moment belongs to us—together. She comes to me with a knowing smile. We hug, and I tell her how proud I am. More than anything I could buy for her, I tell her with my presence that I'll always stand with her—no matter what.

I see my wife in the quiet of our bedroom late at night. The tears flow because of an uncertain future. She needs my love and assurance and I need hers. We openly confess our fears to each other, we pray, and we know that, whatever comes, we'll face it with God and each other. The richest, most successful person in the world cannot buy that sense of peace, joy, and fulfillment.

There's always work to do; it's just not always work that produces public approval or monetary reward. In many ways, that's the most important work a man or woman can be called to do. The beauty is that the person who has retired still has this important work to do, as does the man who has become ill and the woman who has lost the love of her life. Those who are handicapped are called equally to participate in this work. The woman who decides to stay home with her children, and the woman who decides to pursue a career are both called to it.

The bottom line is that God calls each one of us to believe. In believing, we receive grace and understanding so we can know what really matters. Then we have something of great value to share with those we love. With God's help, we work alongside the Almighty. That's good work. That's meaningful work. That's work that can change relationships, pour hope into hopeless lives, and provide a true sense of importance and value. We can all do such work as long as we draw breath—and it will define us long after we are gone.

In *When Work Doesn't Work Anymore,* Elizabeth McKenna writes "To me my father's success was so bright that I lived by its reflected light. I could tell my friends' parents what my father did and see approval in their eyes, not just of him but of me too. It was very clear that his success defined him and took care of me. In return he gave his career his all."[2]

McKenna continues, "From my father I learned about the values of success.... I learned that the nights away from home and late evenings at the office were part of the bargain made for identity and security. A price my father seemed content to pay; a price he expected to pay. My father went to work as a form of love—to give me a better life than he'd had, to give me everything I wanted or needed. I appreciated the trade: my father's physical presence withheld for the noblest of causes—my happiness and well-being. I believed that his success and the quality of my life were deeply linked. I saw that it was okay for work to be impor-tant. *Just as important as I was"* (my emphasis).[3]

WHAT WILL

YOUR FAMILY

SAY WHEN

YOU'RE GONE?

With all due respect to Ms. McKenna, I don't see it that way. I see that choice as a Faustian bargain, as selling one's soul, or at least one's family, for material success.

Nothing can be as important as giving ourselves to those we love. Nothing should ever be as impor-tant as our relationship to God and to those he has given us to love and be loved by. That *is* the most sig-nificant thing we have to offer! Jesus clearly taught that the two most important priorities in life are:

Love the Lord your God with all your
heart, and with all your soul, and with all
your strength, and with all your mind;
and your neighbor as yourself.
(Luke 10:27)

That lesson, taught by Jesus himself, contains the
clearest path to significance—even when trouble
comes and we feel lost. It's all we need to know to go
forward through difficult times. It's the prescription
for healing and well-being and the guideline to pushing on with hope.

What will your family say
when you're gone? "I hardly
knew him, but he gave us everything we needed." Or, "He was
always there. We went through so
many things together. He'll
always be with me." Will they say,
"After Dad died, Mom just
pulled into herself and never
came out again"? Will they say,
"Dad used to be so full of life, but after he was
asked to retire, he lost his joy"? Will they say, "After
the accident, Mom/Dad just stopped living"? Will
they remember how a bitter divorce, a severe illness,
or some other tragic misfortune snuffed out the

> ☙
>
> "DAD, LOOK, I
> WANT TO HELP.
> PLEASE. LET
> ME HELP."

person you once were? The time to think about that is now, while you can still do something about it. Don't wait for that final day when all you have left is the rearview mirror.

၈

I sat in front of my house on a warm late-summer afternoon. The medication had taken a toll, and I was weak both physically and mentally. The exhaustion was so heavy that it seemed almost impossible to move. I was tired of fighting and tired of trying. My son's car pulled into the driveway. I was surprised to see him home. He'd left for his second year of college a few weeks earlier and wasn't expected back yet.

"Hey, Dad," he said with a lilt in his voice. His step was light as he walked briskly up the walkway. "I forgot a few things, so I thought I'd make a quick trip to pick them up."

"Hi, Nick," I said, trying to hold back the emotions that were simmering barely beneath the surface.

"What's up? Just sitting out in the sun?" he asked, smiling confidently.

My lip quivered, and a few tears ran down my cheeks. He hadn't noticed the sadness in my eyes because they were hidden behind sunglasses. But he noticed the tears.

"Dad, what's the matter?" he asked.

"Oh, it's nothing, Nick," I said.

"C'mon, Dad. Don't be a hero. What's going on?"

"I don't know, Nick. I really don't know," I said, my voice weak and uncertain.

"Did you get bad news or something?" he asked, sitting down on the grass near my chair.

"No. Everything's the same. Maybe that's part of it. This awful routine. I've never felt like this before. I can't find anything to hang on to. I'm tired of fighting. I'm tired of this horrible medicine. I'm tired of not doing anything. I'm just really tired," I choked out.

"Gee, Dad. I didn't know it was that bad," he said with unmistakable sincerity.

"Look, Nick, you need to be thinking about school and studying and all that stuff. Don't worry about me." I tried to sound convincing, but he knew me better, and the father-son bond was too strong to ignore.

"Dad, look, I want to help. Please. Let me help," he said.

It hurt to see him deflated and close to tears. I love him so much and I live to see him and his sister happy. But at that moment, I couldn't hold back the overwhelming despair. It came out in a flood of heaving shoulders and slobbering tears.

My son got up, came over, put his arms around me, and said, "Dad, I love you. Please don't give up." His love was real and unselfish. It was medicine for my aching mind and body.

"Dad, I'll quit school and come home for a year if you want," he said. "I'll get a job. I'll do whatever I can to help you and Mom. Just tell me what you want me to do, and I'll do it."

I stopped crying and found renewed strength in my son's selfless love. God had come near to me in the person of my son. That unconditional love lifted me and gave me the motivation to press on. In that moment, I knew that its power was greater than anything life could throw at me.

God had sent my son to encourage me the way I'd tried to encourage my father many years before. No one will ever convince me God didn't orchestrate that powerful appointment on that warm September afternoon.

But encourage one another day after day,
as long as it is still called "Today."
(Heb. 3:13)

"WHAT DO I REALLY BELIEVE?"

❧

Look at the birds of the air, that they do
not sow, nor reap nor gather into barns,
and yet your heavenly Father feeds
them. Are you not worth much more
than they?

—MATTHEW 6:26

I walked into Dr. Milton's office for my scheduled
six-month visit. This was the second time I'd been
on the interferon treatment, while the first time I'd
been on it for eleven months with less-than-ideal

results. This time, it had been half a year, and rib-avirin had been added. Today, I was supposed to find out whether the treatment was working better than the last time.

"Hi, Nick," Dr. Milton said, smiling. We'd become friends after many serious discussions, several medical procedures, and numerous phone calls. When he asked me to stop calling him Doctor and simply call him Charlie, I knew we'd done away with the impersonal aspects of the doctor-patient relationship.

> I'M EXHAUSTED FROM THE TIME I GET UP UNTIL I GO TO BED.

I'd come alone this time, wanting to spare Dawn the tension of another doctor visit.

"So," I said, trying not to appear overly impatient. "What's the verdict?"

"I'll give you the whole analysis in a minute," he said. "First, tell me how you're feeling."

"You want the truth, Charlie?" I asked rhetorically.

He tilted his head and raised his eyebrows in mock sarcasm. "No, I want you to tell me a lie."

"I feel like death warmed over," I said. "I'm exhausted from the time I get up until I go to bed. My headaches are intense. The joint pain is worse, and I'm not suicidal, but sometimes—"

"Okay, that's a good enough description," he said. "Here's the story. You haven't responded the way I'd hoped. There's some improvement, but not enough to make the treatment worth continuing."

"I have to tell you, I'm disappointed but relieved," I said. "I came here ready to tell you I'd had enough of this medicine, and unless you felt very strongly otherwise, I was going to ask you to stop it."

"Okay, then. We'll stop the treatment. There are new drugs in the pipeline and maybe we'll try something else down the road. For now, I want you to rest and see how you feel off the medicine. I'll see you in a month."

Within a month, I was feeling better—not great, but much better, without the added side effects of very powerful chemical therapy. I recognized a pattern emerging: I felt pretty good in the morning and could do things that required concentration and some energy until about noon. Then if I pushed myself beyond that point, I suffered greatly. If I submitted and rested for the afternoon, I generally felt fairly good in the evening. Little by little, I began to do things like write, spend a few hours helping out at

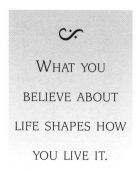

WHAT YOU
BELIEVE ABOUT
LIFE SHAPES HOW
YOU LIVE IT.

the church, and sometimes try a little yard work. That's when I decided I'd put my faith only in God. I wasn't going to ignore the doctors, but their opinions would be weighed in prayer, and I'd trust God to show me what to do and what not to do. Whatever he decided was going to be okay with me.

ᴄ∽

You may think money will solve all your problems. Many have fallen for that trap. The thought process goes like this: Once I've made it, I'll hire other people to do all the things I don't want to do. The problem is there's one thing money can't buy—finding your own purpose and fulfillment in life.

What you believe about life shapes how you live it. The first two questions you have to deal with are: (1) *Where did I come from?* and, (2) *Why am I here?* If you're nothing more than the product of chance, you have to form your impressions about life from that standpoint. If that's the case, your life is just another step in a process heading who

> ᴄ∽
>
> IF YOU FIND YOUR VALUE PLACED BY GOD, THERE'S NO NEED TO LABOR TO "MAKE" YOURSELF VALUABLE.

knows where. Your relationships, desires, and questions are all meaningless. There's nothing except chance, no rules other than what your culture says, no future beyond your stay on earth. It makes no difference what you leave behind, because things will evolve with or without you. With that frame of reference, it's easy to feel worthless.

Maybe you've convinced yourself that achieving enough success to live comfortably is all you need to be happy. Being free to do whatever you want is all there is in that perspective.

Now, consider a God-made reality. According to the Bible, you're made for relationship with your Creator. Your life on earth is only a prelude to an eternity of love, joy, and peace. You, as an individual, matter to God, and he has placed great value in you.

If you labor under the pressure of finding value in and of yourself, you're destined for disappointment. If you find value in others' approval, you're trapped in a vicious cycle that never ends. Approval is very transitory. More is needed, and there's simply never enough. But if you find your value placed by God, there's no need to labor to "make" yourself valuable. You are valuable by nature. The paradox is that you will never feel valuable until you give up trying to do it by your own efforts.

I lived most of my life looking for signs of approval from others. It was hard not to. I realize now it's because I was comfortable with insecurity and self-condemnation. I only believed I was okay when someone said, "Good job." And, of course, every rejection convinced me that I was, in fact, not okay at all. A job failure, a relationship problem, a mistake in judgment ... any and all of these things added to the interior notion that I was not as good as the next person. Then one day, I realized I was trying to measure myself with a yardstick that had all the numbers out of place. No matter how I flipped, turned, or tried again, I would never get an accurate measurement because the yardstick was wrong to begin with.

> ℃
>
> FINDING YOUR WAY TO GOD AND FINDING YOUR TRUE SELF DOESN'T NEGATE LIFE'S TROUBLES.

Here's what I discovered: It's not what we think of ourselves—or what others think of us—that matters. Once that fact is established, a tremendous weight is lifted. All that matters is what our Maker thinks about us. He's the One whose "opinion" is completely valid.

Learning to believe in our true, God-made, valuable self is an important step toward freedom. It's not up to us to increase that value, but to discover what's already been placed in us. The world is no friend to that process. God's Word, his Holy Spirit, and our relationship with Christ (active, ongoing, and personal) are.

Scripture says, "Taste and see that the Lord is good" (Ps. 34:8). That's an invitation. See if God has answers for you. See if he can help you, even help you to believe (see Mark 9:24). You wouldn't have read this far if you weren't searching for something. I believe God is the beginning and the end of your search. Believe in him, and you'll find the way to believe in yourself—regardless of your circumstances.

> ∾
>
> DO YOU BELIEVE YOUR LIFE CAN HAVE MEANING AND PURPOSE AGAIN?

Be advised though—finding your way to God and finding your true self doesn't negate life's troubles.

Coming to terms with the fact that I hadn't responded to treatment wasn't as hard as I thought it would be. I'd begun to talk to God more openly and much more honestly. My walks and prayer times had become much more consoling to me. I admitted my weakness and asked God for the strength to accept a less-than-impressive schedule and to help me live my life with grace and patience. Slowly I began to realize the provisions he had made for me. I had a wonderfully supportive family, a loving church, and enough income to make ends meet. I had at least some strength and some relief from pain so I could do things that helped others—and that always helped me.

With God's help, I began to live my life without the fear of what tomorrow might bring. I started seeking him in every relationship and began to understand that he was very much a part of my life—even the hard parts. Some people call it accepting reality. I prefer to think of it as having the Spirit of God open my eyes to a deeper reality. I guess it's a comfort zone only God can provide. It doesn't negate the pain, but it injects powerful hope into what otherwise might become a hopeless existence.

We all go through many difficulties, because that's the state of this fallen world. But faith in a God who's in control of the ultimate end is a powerful antidote to feelings of hopelessness and insignificance. When we accept the fact that he values us as we are, and when we are set free of the need for approval from others, we find ourselves in a much better position to deal with whatever comes our way.

Stop for a minute: What do you *really* believe? Do you believe your life can have meaning and purpose again? Do you believe God wants to help you achieve that goal? Do you believe he can take the pain in your

life and use it to help someone else? Do you believe
you can find peace again? If not, why not ask God to
help you start your recovery by believing?

> Are not two sparrows sold for a cent? And
> yet not one of them will fall to the
> ground apart from your Father. But the
> very hairs of your head are all numbered.
> So do not fear; you are more valuable
> than many sparrows. (Matt. 10:29–31)

RELATIONSHIP: THE KEY TO SELF-WORTH

We are built for significance. Our problem isn't that we search for it, but that we search for it in all the wrong places.

—JOSEPH STOWELL
Perilous Pursuits

One day the phone rang and a friend from church asked if I'd be willing to help a couple who were having problems. I've been trained as a pastoral counselor, and although it had been some time since I'd accepted any clients, I decided to see if I could help.

"Hello, Frank. This is Nick from church," I said.

"Oh, hi, Nick. How are you doin'?" came the reply.

"I'm fine, Frank. Listen, I got a call from your brother-in-law. He said you and Angela were having a hard time with something, and he thought I might be able to help."

"Well, gee, Nick, I don't want to bother you," he said.

"It's no bother, Frank. I've known you guys for a long time, and if I can help I'd really like to try."

"That would be great, Nick. Angela and I are having a real tough time. We love each other very much, and it's nothing between us, but something is happening to her and she's scared. She doesn't understand it, and so far we can't figure out why she can't eat, she can't sleep—"

"Okay, Frank, why don't you and Angela meet me at the church Wednesday morning? I know you work, but I'm just not too good in the afternoon. Do you think you could come by around ten o'clock?"

"Sure, Nick. We'll be there," he said. "And, Nick, thanks a lot for calling."

What followed was the beginning of an ongoing relationship with two of the most likeable human beings I've ever met. I've been of some help to them, and they've helped me. I began to see God using a lot of what I'd been through to make me better able to understand what they were facing. It soon became clear I could help Angela understand the depression she was slipping into. I could encourage Frank while his wife began to get stronger. I also could offer to stand alongside as a counselor and friend. I could be the person who understood and was able to pray and bring the promises of God to the discussion table. I felt real joy and a sense of purpose.

> ᴄᴦ
>
> I FOUND STRENGTH IN RELATING TO OTHERS AND IN RELATING TO GOD ON THEIR BEHALF.

I found strength in relating to others and in relating to God on their behalf. Getting outside myself was beneficial to me, and in the process I was able to help others.

ᴄᴦ

My illness and how it changed my life had caused me to pull back into myself. Perhaps I had done so in self-defense, thinking I'd be safer alone than in the company of others. Nothing could be further from the truth. Not until I went through the dark passages of isolation and aloneness did I realize how horribly destructive they can be.

God calls us to come out of ourselves. He's a relational being. Since we're created in his image, we're relational beings too. That fact alone reveals so much about who we are and how we can live to the fullest. We are most worthwhile when we're relating first to God and then to others.

What do we do when it's really important for us to understand something? People of all cultures and backgrounds gather information to help them make informed decisions. Most people ask a trusted friend or loved one for their opinion or do research to find out what the experts have to say. They get as many facts together as possible, weigh them, and come to some conclusions. Relationships are complex and often hard to figure out. So why don't we run to God, the only real expert on the subject? When we want to know how to make relationships work, why not consult with the One who invented them?

WHEN WE WANT TO KNOW HOW TO MAKE RELATIONSHIPS WORK, WHY NOT CONSULT WITH THE ONE WHO INVENTED THEM?

Maybe we think he's not available or not interested. Or maybe we get frustrated because the answers aren't always immediate or don't necessarily come the way we expect them. It takes hard, sometimes painful, effort to understand what God made and why he made it. Some of us are afraid to find out that we have big changes to make.

The bottom line is this: We're afraid of the unknown. We know we're hurting, and we need help, but we're not sure we want to open the door to the hard work of discovering the real truth about relationships. In a strange way, it's the "what you don't know can't hurt you" way of thinking. The problem is that what we don't know can't help us either.

> IN OUR CULTURE, SIGNIFICANCE IS MEASURED LESS BY THE CONTRIBUTIONS WE MAKE TO SOCIETY THAN BY OUR POWER, PERFORMANCE, POSITION, AND PROSPERITY.

Do you have a clear picture of how your relationships *should* be, and do you know for certain who defines those *shoulds* in your life? Did you ever wonder if you have a valid picture? In all probability, a composite of outside influences has shaped your concept of who you are and how you should relate to others. Our culture bombards us with images of "successful" relationships—and most of them have to do with taking care of number one. If that isn't what God said—and we know it's not—we're following a road map to a dead end.

According to Joseph Stowell, author and former president of Moody Bible Institute: "The constant refrain we hear is that those who are perceived as significant have arrived and are models of the ultimate pursuit of life. In our culture, significance is measured less by the contributions we make to society than by our power, performance, position, and prosperity."[1]

Stowell's use of the phrase "perceived as significant" is telling. That's exactly what it is—a perception, not a reality. We find true significance in God and in those he has given us to love and be loved by.

Those who have found peace in Christ know that his message is a message of selflessness. Selflessness and significance are inextricably connected. In giving, we receive. In emptying, we are filled. In bowing the knee, we are lifted up. These golden nuggets show us how to relate to one another successfully. Jesus said to those who would listen:

> Blessed are the poor in spirit, for theirs is
> the kingdom of heaven. Blessed are those

who mourn, for they shall be comforted.
Blessed are the gentle, for they shall inherit
the earth. Blessed are those who hunger
and thirst for righteousness, for they shall
be satisfied. Blessed are the merciful, for
they shall receive mercy. Blessed are the
pure in heart, for they shall see God.
Blessed are the peacemakers, for they shall
be called sons of God.
Blessed are those who
have been persecuted
for the sake of righ-
teousness, for theirs is
the kingdom of
heaven. Blessed are you
when people insult you
and persecute you, and
falsely say all kinds of
evil against you because
of Me. Rejoice and be
glad, for your reward
in heaven is great.
(Matt. 5:3–12)

> ❧
>
> MAYBE PURSUING
> OUR DREAMS
> ISN'T ENTIRELY
> OVERVALUED,
> BUT PERHAPS
> EXPERIENCING LIFE
> WITH GOD AND
> OTHERS IS
> UNDERVALUED.

If you've never had an encounter with God, those
words may sound foolish to you. Many think of them
as nothing more than interesting ideas. That's not

what they are. They're among the most important words ever spoken. They're words that have the power to open our eyes to who we were made to be—and how we can have rich and deeply rewarding relationships. We know ourselves better when we see ourselves reflected against those words.

It's hard to hear those words against the backdrop of years of training to the contrary. "Decide what you want and go for it." Most of us have heard, directly or indirectly, that determination is the key virtue. That's not an entirely false concept, but what if we're fooled into wanting the wrong things? What if we spend all our determination on something that takes us nowhere?

Maybe pursuing our dreams isn't entirely overvalued, but perhaps experiencing life with God and others is undervalued. Maybe it's just flipped out of order. Maybe experiencing God and loving relationships will help shape our dreams and give us new ones when some must be left behind.

> ᘓ
>
> "LOVE THE LORD YOUR GOD WITH ALL YOUR HEART, SOUL, AND MIND."

We can all do a better job of balancing our own effort with the virtue of an accessible heart. A heart that's accessible to God and to those we love is in position to bless and be blessed.

Our culture is relentless in giving us a picture of a successful life. It values certain things and disparages others. Prized things are held up to us, and things looked down upon are ridiculed in as many ways. Much of what we see and hear isn't intended to bring us deeper understanding or fulfillment. It's intended to cause us to spend money. As a former advertising executive, I can tell you that most media images are developed to cause people to buy something. It may be a product, or it may be an idea, but the goal is not to inform but to sell. The message is almost always to desire, buy, and consume things we don't have. As a source for understanding our true identity, it's entirely bankrupt.

> ~
>
> YOU'LL FIND THAT THE DOUBT BEGINS TO DISAPPEAR AS YOU EXPERIENCE HIS PRESENCE.

We won't find the key to true and lasting relationships in worldly messages—God alone holds that key. He alone has the answers to every question. All genuine searching to know ourselves and others has to begin with him.

"You shall love the Lord your God with all your heart, and with all your soul, and with all your mind." This is the great and foremost commandment. The second is like it, "You shall love your neighbor as yourself." On these two commandments depend the whole Law and the Prophets. (Matt. 22:37–40)

That Scripture and many others show that God's first call is to relationship—first and foremost with him and then with others around us. It may not be easy. It may not be what we want to hear. It's certainly and reliably in our best interest. Never forget that the Maker understands what he has made better than anyone else does—and that includes us.

God makes it clear that relationships are the central and most significant activity of life. It's where we find true self-worth. First he says, "Love the Lord your God with all your heart, soul, and mind." If we believe that God is a loving Father who wants only what's best for his children, and that he says loving relationships are essential, then it's worth our attention.

> YOUR RELATIONSHIP WITH GOD BEGINS TO GROW WHEN YOU COME TO SEE THE WORLD AS A TEMPORARY HOME.

You may be thinking, *I've just lost the most significant loving relationship I've ever had*. Nothing is more difficult than that, but that's when you need to invest that love in others. It will be a different kind of love, but it will be no less powerful as you redirect it and receive it in return. No matter what your circumstances, you can enjoy loving relationships with God and with those he'll give you to love.

Honest, loving relationships have done more to heal my mind and body than any of the medical treatments I've received. I still take medicine, and I thank God for good physicians. But in my struggle to survive and understand the major change I've experienced, loving relationships have been my greatest help.

᙭

So how do you build a loving relationship with God? Some of the ways are obvious—read his Word, find a community of believers who will help you grow, pray regularly, find experienced believers who can help you when things get tough. There are other ways that aren't as obvious. For example, you can suspend doubt for a few minutes each day; accept wholly that God *is* and that he cares for you, then talk to him from your heart. It's the most sincere form of prayer. Pour out your hurts, your fears, your weaknesses, and your confusion before him. In other words, become vulnerable and allow him to receive you that way. He most certainly will. You'll find that the doubt begins to disappear as you experience his presence. It has been said, "Feed your faith and your doubt will starve."

Another not-so-obvious way to draw closer to God is to examine the difficulties that come your way. Instead of blaming him, ask him to help you see them as part of a bigger picture. Do it honestly, and you'll begin to understand one of life's greatest mysteries. This life has pain and suffering built in because it's fallen. It's not the place God originally created for his children, and no one can expect to get through it without a truckload of trouble. The mystery is that with a heart of faith you can stop trying to make this place something it can never be—heaven on earth. You can resolve to experience this life the way God intends and know that in the end you'll be in a paradise you could never have created for yourself.

When you yield ownership of your life to God, he can bring great gain out of deep pain. He doesn't delight in your pain, but he will redeem it by using it to draw you closer to him—if you let him do so: "And we know that God causes all things to work together for good to those who love God, to those who are called according to his purpose" (Rom. 8:28).

Your relationship with God begins to grow when you come to see the world as a temporary home. It's designed to help you learn about yourself and learn to trust God above all else. Once you achieve that perspective, the world has less power over you. It doesn't become easier, but you're able to approach it with an understanding that only God can give.

Another way to build your relationship with God is by building loving relationships with those around you. By doing so, you're doing what God himself desires to do with all those who are willing. You demonstrate a key characteristic of God when you love others, and through that love you put your foot on the path that leads to healing and wholeness.

Though I don't agree with everything Barbara Kingsolver writes, in her book *Small Wonders* she tells a story that poignantly depicts the power of love. In the book, she teaches her daughter that love is the strongest antidote to evil.

> The closest my heart came to breaking
> was on that day my little girl arrived
> home from school and ran to me, her face
> tense with expectation, asking, "Are they
> still having that war in Afghanistan?" As if
> the world were such a place that in one
> afternoon, while kindergartners were

working hard to master the letter L, it
would decide to lay down its arms. I tried
to keep the tears out of my eyes. I told
her I was sorry, yes, they were still having
the war.[2]

She describes the interaction with her daughter,
then says something I find universally true:

But I understood on that day that we're
all in the same boat. It's the same struggle for each of us, and the same path out:
the utterly simple, infinitely wise, ultimately defiant act of loving one thing and
then another, loving our way back to life.[3]

That statement is also true for you. It's *your* way
back to life.

Love never fails. (1 Cor. 13:8)

Consider It All Joy ... When You Suffer. Yeah, Right!

If you find God with great ease, perhaps it is not God that you have found.

—Thomas Merton

Having your life flipped upside down isn't the worst thing that can happen. But it's not the most comfortable thing either. Like most people, I went through denial, anger, frustration, and finally acceptance. It doesn't have to be a life-threatening illness that causes you to start asking the hard questions. What causes you to feel less than you did before isn't the issue. What's important is how you react to it.

℃

Radio Bible Class publishes a periodical called *Our Daily Bread*. It contains succinct devotionals with Scripture references. One in particular stands out for me.

Italian violinist Niccolò Paganini (1782–1840) was playing a difficult piece of music before a large audience. Suddenly, one string on his violin snapped, yet he continued to play, improvising beautifully. Then two more strings broke, and he completed the composition playing with only one string. When the applause eventually stopped, he nodded at the conductor to begin the encore. The violinist smiled at the audience and shouted, "Paganini ... and one string!" Placing his instrument under his chin, he played again with that one string.[1]

> HAVING YOUR LIFE FLIPPED UPSIDE DOWN ISN'T THE WORST THING THAT CAN HAPPEN. BUT IT'S NOT THE MOST COMFORTABLE THING EITHER.

It's been said that life is 10 percent action and 90 percent reaction. Take, for example, the story of Paul and Silas. As they sat in prison, they prayed and sang praises to God (see Acts 16:25). As a result of their testimony, the jailer and his entire household were converted and baptized. Have you allowed life's adversities to discourage and immobilize you? With God's help, you can start over with the "one string" you have left.

ॐ

"Consider it all joy, my brethren, when you encounter various trials," is James' admonition in James 1:2. He gives his reasons in verses 3 and 4: "knowing that the testing of your faith produces endurance. And let endurance have its perfect result, so that you may be perfect and complete, lacking in nothing."

This isn't a feel-good-for-no-reason philosophy. This isn't acting like Pollyanna or whistling in the dark. James isn't saying that the difficulty itself is joyful, but that what it can produce is joyful. He's encouraging us to consider it joyful that our pain isn't without purpose. The difficulties we go through aren't meaningless, unless we let them

ॐ

JAMES ISN'T SAYING THAT THE DIFFICULTY ITSELF IS JOYFUL, BUT THAT WHAT IT CAN PRODUCE IS JOYFUL.

become so. In other words, he's saying to us, "If you turn this situation into an opportunity to know God better, it can produce great profit that will benefit you for the rest of your life."

A *goad* is a device used to prod, push, or nudge something forward (usually an animal such as a donkey or an ox). Ecclesiastes 12:11 says, "The words of wise men are like goads, and masters of these collections are like well-driven nails; they are given by one Shepherd."

A change in circumstances can act as a "goad"—as a stab with a sharp stick to get us moving. Starting over often forces us to go in directions we don't necessarily want to go. That's where the "goading" comes in. We have no choice. We have to move forward. So we enter a process of growth we would love to avoid but simply can't. In the end, we learn things that make us stronger, better able to handle life's ups and downs; it helps us realize that we can't survive without God's help. We lose some of the foolish notions about handling things on our own and stop thinking we can make all the plans. We start looking up to the God who made us and ask for his help. We humbly submit ourselves to the fact that we are stronger when we depend on God (see 2 Cor. 12:9).

That's what James is talking about when he says that we should "consider it all joy" when we face trials, "knowing that the testing of [our] faith produces endurance," and that we should "let endurance have its perfect result, so that [we] may be perfect and complete, lacking in nothing."

No one relishes suffering. No one waits anxiously for the next trial. It's silly and even masochistic to "enjoy" difficulty. But there's great wisdom in learning that the outcome can be greatly beneficial if we allow God to tutor us through the experience.

გ

I hadn't been in the pulpit in a while, but I was feeling better and I knew it was time. I was scheduled to preach both the 8:30 a.m. and 11:00 a.m. services and I knew it would be draining, yet I felt an assurance of purpose that energized me. Over the years, I've taken many opportunities to preach at our church and others. Though I always experienced a flood of nervous energy before I stepped up to the pulpit, I knew that once I started the Holy Spirit would take my preparation and communicate something meaningful to the listeners.

That morning, I was addressing a group of people who were family as much as congregation. They had called to offer me encouragement again and again. They never tired of including my name on their prayer lists. In one dark time, they took turns driving by to

pray for us. They would pull up to the curb directly in
front of our home, stop and pray, and leave quietly
without coming in—giving new
meaning to the term *drive-by*. It

℃

WHEN I WAS

THROUGH, I HAD

A CALM SENSE

THAT I HAD

ENCOURAGED

THE CHURCH.

was clear they didn't want to dis-
turb us, but they brought
Christ's love near every time
they parked and prayed. More
than once I looked out from the
second-floor bedroom window
with tears of gratitude as I saw
one or another of our dear
friends come to pray.

I don't remember the songs
or the announcements from that morning. I don't
remember what the weather was like or what I was
wearing. What I do remember are the faces.
Expressions of love and goodwill, confidence and
compassion. Expressions of support and the embodi-
ment of Jesus' love.

"Good morning," I began. "Hebrews 11:1 says,
'Now faith is the assurance of things hoped for, the
conviction of things not seen.' This morning, I'd like
to share some thoughts about hope. The Greek word
for *hope* carries the connotation of something that's
definite. It's not a 'maybe.' The hope that God gives
is guaranteed. I'm here this morning to tell you

that—although many things have changed for me, and many of the things I once hoped for have been removed from my life—I'm more hopeful today than I've ever been. I can say that because, through my difficulties, God has shown himself to be faithful. And now my hope is firmly and solely in him."

When I was through, I had a calm sense that I had encouraged the church. It wasn't prideful; it was peaceful. I thanked God for using me to lift up his people. I don't know if I was as clear as I wanted to be, but I do know people were touched by my words because they knew the reality of my life. Things I once perceived as weaknesses they saw as evidence of God's strength.

I did the best I could. I played my one string.

> WHEN WE ALLOW GOD'S LIGHT INTO OUR LIFE WE BEGIN TO SEE WHAT REALLY IS, AND WE ALSO BECOME AWARE OF WHAT IS NOT.

Disappointment often forces us to take close inventory of our beliefs. It may be the only way we'll do the hard work of really looking at our lives. It's a tremendous challenge to move on, to start over with less than we had before. However, it's the only choice that leads to restoration and hope. To put it another way, it's the point where we decide either to play our "one string" or to put the violin down forever.

It's quite normal to question, but eventually we have to move on. We must reach a place where we say, "This is the way it *is*, and I'm going to start again and move forward one step at a time."

In John 16:33, Jesus told his disciples, "These things I have spoken to you, so that in Me you may have peace. In the world you have tribulation, but take courage; I have overcome the world." Those words apply to us today just as much as they did to the early disciples.

I won't tell you I've enjoyed trying harder, but I can say that God has brought good out of what seemed entirely bad. In some ways I'm beginning to see it as a gift, because I'm closer to God and living more peacefully today than I would have been if things had just kept rolling along the way they were. Don't misunderstand me—my life is still full of challenges. Sometimes I wish it weren't so hard. It's just that I have discovered a growing confidence that I can rely on God in every case. I've come to know that God can take what seems entirely awful and use it for good (see Rom. 8:28 NIV).

When we allow God's light into our life we begin to see what really is, and we also become aware of what is not. For example, career, position, power, social acceptability, good looks, and approval seem to offer satisfaction—but in truth, they're always incomplete. God's truth exposes the lies. The challenge is learning not to worship and depend on these things for the satisfaction that only God can give. Ironically, that makes us better able to enjoy them for what they are.

Even more than that, when something good is taken away, when a way of life is no longer possible, when we thought we were doing all the right things but somehow ended up in a hard place ... God is still God. He still comforts those who mourn (see 2 Cor. 1:3–4). He is still the loving Father who cares (see 1 Peter 5:7). He is still the One who never leaves us or forsakes us (see Heb. 13:5).

Adjusting to change is an essential characteristic of life. Everything is always changing, and so must you and I. But one thing that doesn't change is that from the very beginning, God saw each of us as vital and useful. God gives us a position of oversight because he has confidence that we can choose wisely:

> Then God said, "Let Us make man in Our image, according to Our likeness; and let them rule over the fish of the sea and over

the birds of the sky and over the cattle
and over all the earth, and over every
creeping thing that creeps on the earth."
(Gen. 1:26)

And God sees and meets all our needs:

Then the Lord God said, "It is not good
for the man to be alone; I will make him a
helper suitable for him." (Gen. 2:18)

> ↶
>
> SUFFERING,
> DIFFICULTY, HARD
> TIMES—CALL THEM
> WHAT YOU WILL—THE
> EXPERIENCE OF HARD-
> SHIP CAN BE USEFUL.

God intends for us to live in harmony with him. We are to superintend his creation while he superintends our needs. Once, there was no suffering; humankind walked with God in oneness and joy. In his wisdom, however, God gave us free choice. With choice comes the opportunity to obey or to rebel. Adam and Eve chose to rebel. Since that time humans have battled with the choice to accept God's rule or reject it.

The problem is that we're prone to think we can do a better job than God. It's subtle, but we often think we can improve on his plan. The hardest lesson to learn is that our lives are fully formed only in true submission. And most of us struggle to let go.

ᑐ

When the woman saw that the tree was good for food, and that it was a delight to the eyes, and that the tree was desirable to make one wise, she took from its fruit and ate; and she gave also to her husband with her, and he ate. Then the eyes of both of them were opened, and they knew that they were naked; and they sewed fig leaves together and made themselves loin coverings. They heard the sound of the Lord God walking in the garden in the cool of the day, and the man and his wife hid themselves from the presence of the Lord. (Gen. 3:6–8)

> ᑐ
>
> IF YOU FOCUS ON GOD WHO SAVES AND PROTECTS, YOU WILL FIND STRENGTH TO OVERCOME.

Rebellion caused separation and introduced fear and anxiety. This wasn't God's good plan. It was the result of resistance to God's plan.

> ℅
>
> EVEN IN YOUR STRONGEST MOMENTS YOU DON'T HAVE THE STRENGTH TO GO IT ALONE.

Often, in times of difficulty, our first response is to rebel and resist. We expend tremendous energy trying to figure out why this "unfair" situation came upon us. The effort to figure out why never produces anything of value. Realizing that God will walk "through the fire" with us is what really helps (Isa. 43:2). Then we can stop fighting what if and begin to focus on what is. We can focus on the empowering truth instead of the debilitating lie. God has promised to help. He will!

French theologian and author François Fenelon wrote: "Happy indeed are they who bear their sufferings with this simple peace and perfect submission to the will of God! Nothing so shortens and soothes suffering as this spirit of non-resistance."[2]

Suffering, difficulty, hard times—call them what you will—the experience of hardship can be useful. Suffering is the great "attention-getter." In Proverbs 20:30, wise Solomon wrote: "Stripes that wound scour away evil, and strokes reach the innermost parts."

Let me explain what I think that verse means:

"Stripes that wound" may literally refer to lashing with whips and cords (as in Isaiah 53:5 NKJV, "by His [Jesus'] stripes we are healed"). But it can also represent anything that's really painful—something that cuts us deep down and can't be ignored or easily dismissed. In other words, something that demands our attention.

"Scour away evil" is a reference to the possible outcome of going through the painful experience. In other words, the experience itself may help us break through lies, erroneous beliefs, and false hopes. Such things are enemies to the soul and therefore evil. Notice the evil is exposed and "scoured" away. That implies the evil doesn't just fall away; it has to be forced out with effort.

"And strokes reach the innermost parts." The word strokes is obviously another way to describe painful experiences. The writer indicates that anything that hurts deeply has the potential to help significantly. Strokes could be translated "blows," but not necessarily literal blows. It's more unexpected and sudden pain. You've probably heard people say, "That experience must have been quite a blow." I believe that's what Solomon is referring to when he says that such circumstances "reach the innermost parts."

Most of us are afraid of those "innermost parts," but that's where God meets us most intensely. This proverb tells me that though the pain is real and devastating and I can't easily dismiss it or ignore it, I can hope it's leading me to deeper understanding. It tells me that God is aware of the pain, though he doesn't delight in it, and he will meet me where I am completely honest and most vulnerable.

In the end, you're the only one who can determine what you focus on. If you focus on the circumstance you may well be overwhelmed. If you focus on God who saves and protects, you will find strength to overcome.

In *The Purpose Driven Life*, Rick Warren puts it this way: "You will be tested by major changes, delayed promises, impossible problems, unanswered prayers, undeserved criticism, and even senseless tragedies. In my own life I have noticed that God tests my faith through problems, tests my hope by how I handle possessions, and tests my love through people."[3]

In 2 Corinthians 12:10, the apostle Paul wrote: "Therefore I am well content with weaknesses, with insults, with distresses, with persecutions, with difficulties, for Christ's sake; for when I am weak, then I am strong."

On the surface, these words seem to be a contradiction. If you're like me, when you feel weak—you feel weak! You feel that whatever comes next may be more than you can handle. However, even in your strongest moments you don't have the strength to go it alone. When I finally understood that my strength wasn't enough, I found that God's strength is more than enough. That's a guarantee. "For when I am weak, then I am strong." A modern translation might be, "When I'm at the end of my rope I know I need help, so I finally start looking for it." According to Paul, strength is born in weakness— it comes from reaching the end of self-sufficiency. That's the best place to meet God.

Charles Stanley put it this way: "We must learn that it's in our weakest moments that God is free to do his greatest work in empowering and strengthening us. It's in these trying times that we can feel the greatest surge of God's power in our lives. If you're facing an insurmountable trial in your life, do not be afraid to admit that you cannot handle it alone. Instead, confess your weaknesses to the Lord and draw from the deep well of his everlasting strength and love."[4]

Like Paganini, you can turn any situation into an opportunity for good. You can open yourself to God's supernatural abilities. Where you may see no hope, he may see great work to be done. Where you may feel useless, he may have a significant use for you if you'll allow it. Where you may have lost your will to go on, he may be about to reenergize you in a way you couldn't have imagined. If God could make you out of dust, he can certainly use whatever you offer him today. Play your one string. You may be surprised at the beautiful music he'll draw out of it.

Draw near to God and He will draw near to you. (James 4:8)

"Is There No Balm in Gilead?"

Is there no balm in Gilead? Is there no physician there? Why then has not the health of the daughter of my people been restored?

—JEREMIAH 8:22

Recovering from a major challenge is almost never a smooth ride. It would be nice if I could draw a straight upward line to indicate my progress from start to finish—but it wouldn't be true. All that I had been through had taught me a lot, but there was more to learn. I had to be broken further. I thought I had traveled as far down the rings of the inferno as necessary. God had other plans. That's where the detour that saved my life came in.

∽

"I don't know you anymore!" Dawn yelled. "You're not the man I married. I can't stand to be around you."

The words stung and I recoiled, but only for a moment.

"If you could only feel what I feel, you'd get off my back," I snapped. "Go. Just go upstairs. I can't talk to you anymore."

Her eyes flashed anger, but her face was furrowed with pain—the pain of recognition that surfaces when an old problem appears irresolvable. It was the pain that comes with battle fatigue, with fear that the separation between people may be so deep that no amount of talking and no amount of trying can bridge the gap.

> WHEN SHE SAW ME DROP BACK AND ACCEPT DEFEAT, IT KILLED HER EMOTIONALLY AND VERY NEARLY KILLED US.

I stormed off in a self-righteous huff, thinking, *I'm the one suffering. I have these awful chronic migraine headaches, and she can't stop nagging me. I'm exhausted all the time. Doesn't she see that?*

I was hurting physically—that was true. But I was wrong in not seeing how much my wife was suffering emotionally. She'd been patient, loving, and supportive throughout my illness and all the ups and downs. She'd never left my side as I wrestled with giving up my career and adjusting to a different lifestyle. She was fine with giving up the financial status she enjoyed as the wife of a company president.

> IT WAS JUST EASIER TO BLAME SOMETHING OR SOMEONE ELSE, SO THAT'S WHAT I DID.

What she couldn't accept was my giving up on life. When she saw me drop back and accept defeat, it killed her emotionally and very nearly killed us. That's when it all fell apart. She had no patience when it became apparent that I was taking the easy way out. She couldn't tolerate my resignation, my acceptance, my acquiescence, and the plain fact that I'd stopped fighting for the things I loved. She was right—and I was about to find out in the most heart-wrenching way.

It happened slowly—small decision by small decision. Missing a family function because I didn't feel like making the effort. Refusing an opportunity to go for a walk with her. Tiny, seemingly inconsequential decisions that slowly piled up until I'd built up a formidable mound of indifference. Of course, I always had a good self-pitying excuse. After all, I was ill. But the truth was, many times the reason for my decisions was just plain laziness. I could have participated but chose to withdraw. Looking back, it's incomprehensible to me that I didn't realize I was communicating so much by doing so little.

At the time, it was just easier to blame something or someone else, so that's what I did. It wasn't just my wife; I got very lazy with my kids as well. Always justifying. Never taking stock of the effect of my selfish choices. Always assuming we would hold together as a family.

After awhile, I felt misunderstood and Dawn felt betrayed—not the formula for a happy marriage. As we grew apart, increasing emotional pain magnified my perception of physical pain, so I pulled further into myself. That's when I made the biggest mistake of all—I decided it would be easier to stop trying. I thought all that was left was avoiding pain—my attempt at the great escape. I ran from anything uncomfortable and hid in my fortress of unfeeling.

The method of escape is never the issue. The issue is the decision to escape. Anything other than dealing with reality only prolongs the inevitable. We all come slamming down sooner or later. It's always a mistake to escape because we can never escape for good. It's always wise to deal openly, honestly, and humbly with issues, relationships, and circumstances. Left alone, they never get better—only worse.

In my case, I drifted into self-pity. When life is getting tough and problems abound, it's easy to blame everything but self. "This person doesn't understand what I'm going through. That person was insensitive to me. The other person didn't take my situation seriously." For me, self-pity was becoming a way of life. And because of it, I wasn't a pleasant person to be around.

> ONE DAY WE WAKE UP IN A WORLD OF OUR OWN MAKING, A WORLD WE DON'T RECOGNIZE.

It's tempting, because it almost seems to work for a time. But when we get to the point where we even start to withdraw from God, the Holy Spirit begins to groan and our soul begins to die. That's why it's so insidious. Most of us would never choose to kill our own souls. No, we make small choices to do things that will not strengthen our souls. Then, when we lose that deep sense of connection with our spirit—the very center of God's existence in our lives—we find ourselves on the slippery slope. We grow colder and colder. We make decisions that are less and less about our true feelings and more and more about hanging on. Soon, moving further and further away becomes easier and easier. One day we wake up in a world of our own making, a world we don't recognize.

For me, reality hit when I realized I was drifting away from the three people I love most in the world—my wife, my son, and my daughter.

One afternoon, after an unsatisfying conversation with my son, I felt a terrible sense of loss. What happened to the closeness we once had? I asked God what was going on. I figured it was not unusual to have ups and downs in marriage, but up to then I'd had an open channel with my son. Now it seemed blocked, strained, uncomfortable.

I have no illusions about my kids. They're great, but I don't make them out to be perfect. They make mistakes and have strengths and weaknesses like all other human beings. But my kids are now in their twenties, and they're easy to be proud of. Nick is solidly committed to his faith. He works hard at his church and has been on mission trips. He studies and teaches God's Word. There's plenty of evidence he's doing his best to follow God faithfully. So I couldn't lay the blame on him. Somewhere down inside, I knew it had to be me.

And then there's Danielle. My daughter has the biggest heart and has always championed the underdog—maybe because she had a tough time in school and her confidence was shaken at an early age. She always sees the plight of the person others cast aside. In grade school, she proudly walked beside the wheelchair-bound little boy when the other kids ran away from him. She'd be the first to stick up for the kid who was picked on. In high school, any kids who had problems were welcomed in our home. She'd bring them home to us like stray puppies. She helped a young girl who lost her mother in a car accident. That same girl betrayed her years later, and Danielle found the grace to forgive her. That's the kind of heart God gave her.

I KNEW SHE WAS LONELY AND UNSURE ABOUT LIFE. AND ALL I COULD DO WAS LIE IN BED AND WATCH THE WORLD GO BY.

Danielle was dealing with some personal issues, and the stress of the situation escalated into panic and anxiety. Often, she'd collapse in my arms sobbing, asking for help. It broke my heart that I couldn't make her pain go away. But what also chipped away at my soul was that I wasn't fully able to give myself to her. Part of me was held back under the anguish and guilt of serving the god of escape. Even when we have good intentions, if we're in a broken relationship with God we can't be strong—really strong. The power that comes from serving God with our whole heart is short-circuited, and though we can do loving things, our ability to love freely is compromised. So I gave my Danielle all I had to give, but I knew she deserved more from me. One occasion tore me apart.

> I ASKED GOD TO WALK ME THROUGH THE VALLEY THAT LAY AHEAD.

Knock. Knock. "Dad, can I come in?" she asked from the upstairs hallway.

"Sure, come on in," I said. It was eleven o'clock in the morning, and I was in bed, watching some boring cable news channel.

"Bad headache already?" she asked.

"Yeah, it started early today," I answered.

She sat on the edge of the bed and made small talk. I knew she was trying to comfort me and give me a little company. I remember apologizing for being a downer.

"Stop it, Dad," she said. "It's not your fault. I love you. Hang in there."

As the door closed behind her, I welled up with tears. Here was my hurting twenty-one-year-old daughter trying to encourage me. I knew she was lonely and unsure about life. And all I could do was lie in bed and watch the world go by. I had almost forgotten how to stand up and fight.

ᠭᠣ

So there I was. Worn-out platitudes and cross-stitched mottoes wouldn't cut it. Simplistic answers were of no use to me. I knew I was dangerously close to losing major ground. I knew I had to travel to the depths of my soul and find the will to fight—fight for those I loved and for my relationship with the Lord. I realized that I had to start over. I had substituted one false identity for another, and God was again knocking at the door of my heart.

Yes, I knew God would help me. Yes, I knew his power was essential if I was to have any hope of victory. Without it, there was no chance to hang on to the ones I loved. No chance for me to reestablish a life-giving bond with the One who died so I could be free and who suffered so I could find help in this difficult journey called life.

So I began to fight in the only way that made sense. I fell on my face and begged God to forgive me for trying to do it my way. I openly admitted that I had dethroned him in favor of making things "easier." At least I thought I was making them easier—when all the while I was complicating them to the extreme. I confessed to him that I had rationalized an easy way out because I had been dealt a tough hand. After all, I was forced to withdraw from my career, live with pain, and start over when I thought I would be just beginning to coast. I asked his forgiveness for focusing on what I had lost and forgetting all he had provided. It was a bitter, tear-filled confession, and it was humbling to see myself without excuse or defense. The words of the old hymn that closes every Billy Graham meeting were absolutely appropriate for the meeting I had with God that night: "Just as I am, without one plea."[1]

And so I asked God to walk me through the valley that lay ahead. I knew it would be difficult to face the truth—I had become a coward. I just didn't want to fight anymore. The details of the battle aren't really important. The bottom line is: When my strength wasn't enough—his was.

One particular night about 2:00 a.m., I cried out to him, "Father, please have mercy." It wasn't the first or the tenth or the hundredth time I'd uttered those words. But this time, as Rita Springer sang prayers in the background, I looked out the window into the black night. As I did, words formed in my mind, *Is there no balm in Gilead?* I didn't really understand the reference, but it was clearly impressed on my heart. Throughout the night the phrase was never far from my consciousness.

Next morning, I called a good friend and brother in the Lord. "Dick, where do I find the phrase about a 'balm in Gilead' in the Bible?"

"That's Jeremiah," he said. "Let me think a second. Wait, I have my Bible here. Let's see. That's in Jeremiah 8:22."

I thanked him and read the context of that verse. Jeremiah, speaking as a prophet of the Lord, is asking God's people why they're not taking advantage of God's help. In fact, God is hurting for his people because they're not receiving the help he wants to give them.

> My sorrow is beyond healing, My heart is faint within me! Behold, listen! The cry of the daughter of my people from a distant land:

"Is the Lord not in Zion? Is her King not within her?"

"Why have they provoked Me with their graven images, with foreign idols?"

"Harvest is past, summer is ended, And we are not saved."

For the brokenness of the daughter of my people I am broken; I mourn, dismay has taken hold of me. Is there no balm in Gilead? Is there no physician there? Why then has not the health of the daughter of my people been restored? (Jer. 8:18–22)

> ☙
>
> PAIN, FEAR, AND THE SPECTER OF GREAT LOSS HAD FORCED ME TO SEEK HIM ONCE AGAIN.

I knew what God was saying to me. He was asking me, "Nick, don't you believe I can help you? Don't you believe the healing of your soul is in my power? Don't you know it has always been there?" Humbled and broken, I had to admit that I had pushed aside the help that God's hand had extended to me. Somehow I thought he could help others, but the time had passed for me. My family and I had prayed for healing for a long time and nothing had changed. I had accepted that God didn't have my answer, and so I had left him on the shelf. Somehow I had made him god with a small *g*. But that isn't who he is!

Pain, fear, and the specter of great loss had forced me to seek him once again. I'm not talking about an intellectual pursuit. That wasn't nearly enough. I had to pursue him with a desperate heart that was open to his ways and  wasn't limiting. I had to pursue him like the deer David wrote about in Psalm 42:1. I was dying of thirst and needed a drink only God could give. I was "pant[ing] for the water brooks" and the Lord offered me water from a well deeper than anyone has ever dug.

The next night as I prayed, the phrase came to me again, *Is there no balm in Gilead?* And this time I knew God was reminding me of a call I had accepted years earlier to minister to his sheep. Now God was asking me if I would pick up the call—this time. Looking out into the dark night, I could see people who had affirmed my call years before. I could see the hurt, pain, and difficulties of their lives. I could see their need for help. And I could hear God asking me, "Will you bring the balm of Gilead to my people? Will you take up the call that you laid aside?" "Yes, Lord, I will. Help me to know how, where, and when."

Something clicked, like a piece of machinery that moves in short steps until it hits the spot where it fits and drops into place. Something dropped into place in my heart and soul. I sensed that God was working, and that I had important things to do with my life.

There was no sense of condemnation. There was no sense of God's displeasure. There was only affirmation: "This is the way laid out for you." I didn't have a giddy sense of discovery. I had a much deeper realization that God works in wondrous and mysterious ways. I had no illusions that life would suddenly become easy, but I knew God was demonstrating in real and concrete terms that he is true to his Word. If we use what faith we have to diligently seek him, he won't fail to reveal himself: "Without faith it is impossible to please Him, for he who comes to God must believe that He is and that He is a rewarder of those who seek Him" (Heb. 11:6).

∾

A few weeks later, I was asked to read Scripture in church. Unable to contain myself, I shared a little about God's goodness before I read. One of the elders came to me when I returned to my seat.

"I'm supposed to preach next week," Armand said. "You seem like you have more to say. Do you want to take my turn?"

"Yes. Yes I do, Armand," I said.

He nodded, smiled, and went back to his seat.

The following week, I took the pulpit and laid out the whole story for my church family. I was as honest as I could be. There were tears, and there was exultation at God's glorious mercy. People were touched—not by my eloquence but by the witness of God's faithfulness.

THE ONLY WAY TO TRULY KNOW MYSELF IS TO SEE MYSELF THROUGH HIS EYES.

I told them about the balm in Gilead. I told them I was 100 percent sure that God had healed my soul and done a magnificent work of mercy and grace in the part of me that was the sickest. I told them that my body seemed better and perhaps had been touched as well.

As I stood in the pulpit and looked over the congregation, my eyes filled with tears of joy. There sat Dawn, Nicholas, and Danielle smiling up at me. As I shared my heart, walls were coming down. I could feel that hearts had been opened and that we were on the right path as a family.

So now, when I think about a fresh start, I look at it differently. I'm not the person who was identified by a title or by roles in life. I'm not even the person who thought he had come to grips with life-changing circumstances. I'm just a simple man, made by an awesome Creator. I'm a man in a relationship with the God who loves me and cares about all the things that should be important to me, a man coming to know the God who stuck by me even when my decisions weren't the best.

I have seen the value in trusting God and, most important, I have come to know that the only way to truly know myself is to see myself through his eyes.

The good news is that he knows you—no matter what you've been through or are going through. He knows you and loves you with the most empowering love imaginable. Only God knows how to help you start over. So, my friend, my advice is this: Ask God to show you how to go forward from this point on. Genuinely asking for his help is the beginning of a process. There will be twists and turns, but the end is assured. He only leads to better places. The challenge is to continue to follow even when you don't yet see where he's taking you.

Don't fall for shortcuts. There's no escape from the truth. We are surrounded with opportunities to escape into things that appear to be good, but in fact are dead ends. The good news is that God doesn't care which escape we've chosen. There's no hierarchy of bad, really bad, and the worst possible. It's all rebellion, missing the mark, futile. There is no escape from reality, because reality is where God is—and, like it or not, it's where he waits for each one of us.

There is a balm in Gilead. There is help for every person who is willing to believe. And that's my message to you through this book. No matter what change you are going through or have gone through, there IS a balm in Gilead, if you will only believe it and receive it.

I do believe; help my unbelief.
(Mark 9:24)

12

It's Really
Up to You

ॐ

The doors stood open, but the captives
had forgotten how to get out.

—EDITH WHARTON
The House of Mirth

I stayed away from my former business, GP&P, for
the most part. The G still stood for Gugliotti, but
while I'd once been a significant presence, I was now
nothing more than a memory for most of the
employees. It had been a couple of years since I'd set
foot in the door. The welcome mat was always out

for me, but it felt better to let it alone. It was too personal and too hard to be there and yet not be part of all that was going on.

On this particular afternoon, I was asked to come back to consult with a client. The offer to do so had always been there, but I had always declined because a condition of my disability insurance was that I couldn't earn money. Maybe it was boredom. Maybe I needed to feel needed. Whatever the reason, I accepted this time. I wasn't going to get paid, so money wasn't the motivation.

I was to visit the client and conduct an interview, then make advertising and marketing recommendations. It was something I'd done hundreds of times in more than twenty years as a marketing consultant. But this time, it didn't feel right.

The interview went well, and determining the best course of action wasn't difficult. But I felt like a foreigner. Where I'd once relished the ease with which I could make a client feel relaxed, now I just didn't like the game that had to be played. The whole encounter felt contrived. The people were nice, the tour of their facility was fine, drawing out their goals was easy enough—but the process seemed phony to me. It never had before. And it wasn't because the interaction between client and consultant isn't perfectly acceptable. It was something in me that was different.

It wasn't a matter of pride; it was a realization that the time for me to do that kind of work had passed.

Looking back, I believe God helped me to change because I needed to change. I couldn't have dealt with my new reality if I didn't. I was, in fact, no longer the person I'd been before. I'm not saying that I became somehow better than those who feel comfortable in that setting. I'm saying, for me, I had to move on.

Dawn didn't want me to take the assignment. She knew instinctively it wouldn't be a good fit anymore. Being too stubborn for my own good, I had to learn for myself. In the end, I couldn't wait to be done with the job.

> ℘
>
> I REALIZED THAT A CHAPTER OF MY LIFE WAS TRULY OVER AND THAT I'D NEVER GO BACK EVEN IF I COULD.

It was a turning point for me. I realized that a chapter of my life was truly over and that I'd never go back even if I could. The doors to the prison of self-pity were forever blown off. I no longer felt grief over the loss of my career and the position I thought defined me.

Is something holding you in prison? Something you think you can't overcome? Does something make you feel powerless? It may be nothing more than inertia. It takes energy to get started in another direction. When you come to grips with a new choice and allow God to lead you forward, those prison doors fly open. Even after they're open, however, you still have to put one foot in front of the other and walk out.

> ⌒
>
> THE DOORS ARE
> OPEN, BUT YOU
> MUST CHOOSE
> TO GET OUT
> OF YOUR
> PARTICULAR
> PRISON.

⌒

Trusting God is the single most freeing decision you can make. It frees you from trying to figure things out on your own and the limits of man-made plans. It gives you back today, which you may have mortgaged for an imaginary tomorrow. God has made a way, but you must choose to follow him. The doors are open, but you must choose to get out of your particular prison.

God not only created mankind, he superintends his creation. After the fall, he made a way for us to get back where we ultimately belong. Although it may be difficult, we still have the option to choose freedom over slavery. Nothing can stop us. Viktor Frankl, author of *Man's Search for Meaning,* put it in the following terms. Held in a Nazi concentration camp, he was stripped of friends, family, and finally even his clothes. He later wrote that his captors could take everything away, and still they couldn't take away his freedom to choose how he would react to his circumstances.[1]

You have to get up and walk out of the prison of self-reliance or the prison of self-pity. You must venture into the freedom of reliance on God. I don't believe it's a choice based on "figuring God out." I believe it's a choice made in response to the "gentle whisper" of his voice (1 Kings 19:12 NIV). It's the voice of a father calling his lost child: "Then the Lord God called to the man, and said to him, 'Where are you?'" (Gen. 3:9). The freeing response is, "Here I am, Lord." The freeing response is to trust. Trust leads to faith. Even the smallest bit of faith is enough, because it contains within it all that's needed to get up and walk out of prison.

You walk out to change your relationship to the world around you. You walk into the most important relationship of your life, a relationship with your Maker. From that relationship comes the guidance to move away from darkness and straight into light.

Trust in the Lord with all your heart and
do not lean on your own understanding.

In all your ways acknowledge Him, and
He will make your paths straight.
(Prov. 3:5–6)

In principle it sounds easy enough—trust the
God who made you. In practice it involves a life-
and-death battle. You learn to die to your ways and
live in the truth of God's ways. It's not easy—if it
were, it wouldn't require a cross. There's no such
thing as cheap grace. God paid a price, and so must
you. It's not the same price
Christ paid for us, but it's significant nonetheless. In the
end, it's worth more than you
imagine. You find the answers
to all your important questions, peace that passes
understanding, and the assurance that will steady you in
good times and bad.

"GOD IS THE
ONLY ONE WHO
CAN SEE AROUND
CORNERS!"

One of the first things you'll have to battle is the
discomfort of giving up control. As long as you
think you have control, you'll want to hang on to
the imagined security of managing the outcome. I
used to think I had to be in control to be safe—until
I learned that the safest place I can be is in submission to God.

The Bible, in many ways, is a record of man's inability to move toward wholeness, goodness, and even happiness without God's intervening grace. When left to his own devices, man filled the earth with violence and corruption (see Gen. 6:12–13). It's in our best interest to give up control. God alone is able to be the Prime Mover. His wisdom is far greater than ours. It's not a burden to give him control; it's a privilege.

> ℃
>
> WE HAVE TO WORK HARD AT DEVELOPING A DEEPLY EMPOWERING RELATIONSHIP WITH GOD.

The misunderstanding about control starts with a faulty premise: the notion that we can control the circumstances of our life. Sure, we can control some things, but everyone has unexpected events come into their life. Does anyone ever control life and death, sickness and health, aging, or unseen circumstances that simply "happen"? Even people who seem to achieve everything they set out to accomplish face many things that are beyond their control. I always tell my daughter, "God is the only One who can see around corners!"

That's not a frightening or denigrating thought. It shines a bright light on God's significance and tells us about ourselves as well. God has chosen only mankind to share in his eternal plan. We are not insignificant. We are "fearfully and wonderfully made" (Ps. 139:14), but we are not God. He invites us to give him control and participate in the working out of his plan. It's a marvelous invitation. It validates us more than anything we can ever accomplish on our own.

So it's not really about giving up control; it's about giving up the fantasy of control. Submitting to God's control is a sign of maturity and wisdom, not weakness. In *The Worth of a Man,* Dave Dravecky says, "I think most men are afraid of showing their weakness because it causes them to lose control. When I was in baseball, I talked very little about what was going on in my heart with the guys in the clubhouse. To open up like that was a sign of weakness, and to show weakness means to lose control. Ballplayers don't dare make themselves vulnerable. They don't expose their weakness."[2]

Dravecky learned to give up control—he had to. A major league pitcher has to learn a lot about life when his pitching arm has to be removed due to cancer. Dravecky's idiom is professional baseball, and he draws from his experiences in that arena. What he says holds true for all of us. Making our plans and taking control of our lives is building on shaky ground. No one knows what tomorrow will bring.

Don't misunderstand me. I'm not suggesting that we sit back and do nothing. I'm suggesting an active process. We have to work hard at developing a deeply empowering relationship with God. It's anything but passive. We "work out [our] salvation with fear and trembling" (Phil. 2:12). It's hard, good, and absolutely essential work—but it's not working on a plan of our own making. It's not determining what circumstances will be most productive or deriving personal value by what is considered to be acceptable accomplishment. It's discovering how to be used to further the work God is doing.

> SOMEHOW HE KNEW THERE WAS A POWERFUL PRESENCE IN THE SKY AND THE TREES AND EVEN THE BIRDS THAT FLEW BY.

God can use you right where you are, just the way you are. You may have thought you were at the end. The truth is you're at a beginning.

Oswald Chambers wrote, "A follower of God must stand so very much alone that he never realizes he's alone. In early stages of Christian life, disappointments come—people who used to be lights flicker out, and those who used to stand with us turn away. We have to get so used to it that we will not even realize we're standing alone."[3]

The apostle Paul wrote, "No one stood with me, but all forsook me.... But the Lord stood with me and strengthened me" (2 Tim. 4:16–17 NKJV).

When you realize you're alone, you begin the painful process of separating from false hopes. Only then do you have room for the One who never disappoints: "for He Himself has said, 'I will never desert you, nor will I ever forsake you'" (Heb. 13:5).

Only then are you able to see the One who truly does walk alongside—leading, guiding, and protecting: "For you were continually straying like sheep, but now you have returned to the Shepherd and Guardian of your souls" (1 Peter 2:25).

In this world, you walk as an individual. In his kingdom, "the Father of mercies and God of all comfort" (2 Cor. 1:3) always walks with you. Understanding that he alone can fill the empty places in your heart is the beginning of the most powerful healing of all.

ᵕ

One day, a man walked to the top of a lonely hill. Each step reverberated in the hollowness of his heart. He was desperate under the weight of his own sorrow.

He was alone. He felt utterly forsaken. A nearby stream flowed steadily, reminding him that the world wouldn't stop because of his suffering. The stream would run into the river and the river into the ocean as it always had. The thought made him aware that the world would go on without him and he would hardly be missed.

Falling to his knees, he covered his eyes with his hands. Bitter tears poured down his face. Unable to find a hopeful thought, he felt the little strength he had slipping away. Agonizing moments passed before he stood and lifted his hands toward heaven. From the deepest part of his soul, he cried out:

"Why, God? Please tell me why!"

He heard no sound but the breeze rustling the trees. There was no voice from the clouds. He was utterly alone—or was he? He bowed his head and emptied his heart. Then he just sat in the grass wondering. Slowly, he sensed he wasn't alone. Somehow he knew there was a powerful presence in the sky and the trees and even the birds that flew by. Somehow he knew God was there.

He came down from that mountain on more than his own power. A deep reassurance pushed him onward. He didn't come away with immediate answers, but with lingering questions. He also came down with a small spark of hope, and that was what he needed most. His cry hadn't gone unanswered!

I know that man well—he's with me everywhere
I go.

> I call heaven and earth to witness against
> you today, that I have set before you life
> and death, the blessing and the curse. So
> choose life in order that you may live, you
> and your descendants. (Deut. 30:19)

13

STARTING OVER: SEVEN SUGGESTIONS TO HELP YOU GET GOING

༄

He has the deed half done who has made
a beginning.

—HORACE

The sun was shining the day we went to Sam and
Jackie's for a picnic. G. and Yolanda were there.
P. J., Dawn, Danielle, Shaun, Britt, John, the
Chabots, Pastor John and Carmela, and a whole
bunch of kids also came. Someone got the idea that
a basketball game would be fun. Using very little

wisdom, I decided to play. As the game went along,
I tired before the younger folks did.

"Hey, Moses!" Pastor John shouted.

"Okay," I said. "I admit it. I can't keep up with
these young kids."

The nickname stuck. I don't mind. It's all in fun,
but I've decided to try to get them to call me
Lazarus instead. After all, the doctors told me I had
five years to live ... and that was
twenty years ago. And I've been
sick a few times when it looked
like the end was near. But each
time the Lord raised me up. So,
I think Lazarus fits better.
Believe me when I say I'm
grateful to God that I'm still
here to be teased by friends.

> ෬
>
> GOD RAISED ME
> FROM THE PIT—
> AND HE WILL
> SURELY DO THE
> SAME FOR YOU.

God raised me from the pit—
and he will surely do the same for you. I encourage you
to start today. Don't wait. There will never be a better
time. You will never be more prepared. It will never be
any easier. Take the first step. Ask our Lord to accom-
pany you on your journey. He promised he would, and
he never breaks a promise. As Hebrews 13:5–6 says,
"For He Himself has said, 'I will never desert you, nor
will I ever forsake you,' so that we confidently say, 'The
Lord is my helper, I will not be afraid.'"

ᵔ

Here are several steps that helped me along the way. I hope they help you too.

1. ASK GOD FOR HELP

The first thing you need to do is admit your need. It sounds simplistic, but it's critical. "The fear of the Lord is the beginning of wisdom, and the knowledge of the Holy One is understanding" (Prov. 9:10).

Because God sees the big picture, he alone knows all the details of your life. You are limited to a finite understanding of what you see, but God has no such limitation. His wisdom is more complete than yours. He knows things you only think you understand. God waits for you to say, "Lord, I believe you have the answers. I openly confess my weakness and ask you to lead me out of this hard place."

YOU CAN PRAY, "LORD, TAKE THIS CUP FROM ME." BUT YOU SHOULD ALSO PRAY, "YET NOT MY WILL BUT YOURS BE DONE."

James 4:10 reads, "Humble yourselves before
the Lord, and he will lift you up" (NIV). Jesus
demonstrated the power of humility. He showed us
that good comes from faithfulness—even in suffering. He didn't escape the suffering. Instead, he
turned to his heavenly Father in reliance on him.
You must do the same.

You can pray, "Lord, take this cup from me."
But you should also pray, "Yet not my will but yours
be done." And, "God, give me the grace I need to
live my life trusting you above my circumstances."

It's natural to want to be happy. In his book
Shattered Dreams, Larry Crabb puts it this way: "We
can't stop wanting to be happy. And that urge
should prompt no apology. We were created for
happiness. Our souls therefore long for whatever we
think will provide the greatest possible pleasure. We
just aren't yet aware that an intimate relationship
with God is that greatest pleasure."[1]

Your hope will break through when you stop listening to the negative voice in your head and begin
to hear God's voice. Peter reiterates James' words:
"Humble yourselves under the mighty hand of
God, that He may exalt you at the proper time"
(1 Peter 5:6).

2. BE AWARE THAT GOOD CONSEQUENCES CAN COME FROM BAD CIRCUMSTANCES

"How can you talk about good when I'm feeling so bad?" That's a fair question. The answer has to do with who defines the word good. When you yield to God's definition of good, all the parameters change. Romans 8:28 probably is quoted as often as any Scripture—and may have been misused as much as any Scripture: "And we know that God causes all things to work together for good to those who love God, to those who are called according to His purpose."

> YOU TRULY DEMONSTRATE YOUR LOVE FOR GOD WHEN YOU LOVE HIM IN YOUR SUFFERING.

When that verse is used to convey a philosophy of "grin and bear it," it's insensitive and insulting. This verse is more than a Band-Aid. It has God's supernatural power to soothe and comfort. It's not the power of the words; it's the power of the truth behind the words.

The truth of that Scripture has often been trivialized. In it Paul is reminding the Roman church of their ultimate position in Christ. His message is that God, in Christ, has made the way for peace, truth, hope, and eternal assurance. Therefore, if you stand in faith, if you "love God" and "are called according to His purpose," God promises to help you make sense of things that otherwise seem senseless. I've seen the crushing weight of bad circumstances break open seeds that brought forth new life.

You truly demonstrate your love for God when you love him in your suffering. If you love him in trial and tribulation—then you really do love him. God doesn't put you in trouble to see if you love him. The world does a fine job of that on its own. You, however, have a unique opportunity to find out for yourself how trustworthy God really is.

Job, after great trials, was able to say: "Naked I came from my mother's womb, and naked I shall return there. The Lord gave and the Lord has taken away. Blessed be the name of the Lord" (Job 1:21).

God isn't asking you to be Job. He's asking you to trust him to get you through. He's inviting you to lay your suffering at his feet and allow him to help you carry your burden. He's inviting you to take his hand. Isaiah clearly knew this truth when he recorded God's thoughts:

> You are My servant, I have chosen you
> and not rejected you. Do not fear, for I
> am with you; do not anxiously look

about you, for I am your God. I will strengthen you, surely I will help you, surely I will uphold you with My righteous right hand. (Isa. 41:9–10)

An effective prayer might be, "While I yet suffer, I will trust you, Lord. I will trust you for the outcome and the timing. Help me to be confident that somehow you'll bring something good out of this hard circumstance."

> ℘
>
> "PRAYER SHOULD BE A TIME OF NO-HOLDS-BARRED, STRAIGHT-AHEAD COMMUNICATION WITH GOD."

It's not easy to look at feelings of depression, despair, or loss as good things. But if the pain softens your heart and causes you to look to God for help, it becomes a catalyst for something of exceptional value. In some ways, suffering is a gateway to abundant life. I'm not making light of your suffering—I suffer too. I'm just saying there can be profound meaning in it. God can use it to open your heart to things it otherwise wouldn't be open to.

3. Plug in to Prayer

The power of prayer can't be overstated. In good times, prayer is easily taken for granted. Often that's because it's misunderstood. Prayer is much more than the offering up of a "laundry list" of your requests. It's a divinely instituted channel through which you engage almighty God—not because of the eloquence of your words or the intensity of your demeanor, but because of the openness of your heart before the One who listens and responds "generously and without reproach" (James 1:5).

David Jeremiah puts it this way: "Prayer should be a time of no-holds-barred, straight-ahead communication with God. We cut to the root of the problem, and we're not afraid to name names. And when that happens, we feel a tremendous sense of unburdening ourselves before the most intimate Friend imaginable. He's listening, he cares, he responds, and we can tell him anything at all."[2]

Throw human logic and traditional forms aside. God has said we're to cast all our care upon him—period (see 1 Peter 5:7 NKJV). If we hold back, we short-circuit prayer's healing power and deflect truths we need to face honestly in the unfiltered light of God's presence.

Prayer changes people as much as it changes circumstances. Of course, God has the power to change circumstances and does so regularly. But he also changes the praying person—for the better. A person who truly communes with God in prayer comes away renewed and better able to meet life's challenges. Prayer quiets the heart and soothes the mind. It's nothing short of a portal to intimacy with God, and no one can be close to God and remain unchanged. The power of God's presence adjusts moods, attitudes, and—perhaps most important—perspectives.

The very direction of prayer is instructive. It's directed to God, who's bigger, more able, and wiser than we are. Realizing that God is all-powerful and willing to bring that power to bear on our life is a tremendous comfort. The only stipulation is that we trust him to work things out his way. God wants to make our true value known to us. One way he does it is through the reciprocal activity of prayer.

> ℘
>
> SPEAK TO GOD BY ALL MEANS, BUT LISTEN AS WELL. HE WON'T FAIL TO REACH THE INNER-MOST PARTS OF YOUR HEART.

For a long time, I thought prayer was talking to God, but that's only part of it. Prayer is listening to God as well. I've never heard his voice the same way I hear my wife's voice, but I've heard in my heart and spirit assuring thoughts that I came to recognize were not of my own making. Sometimes praying with God's Word in front of me brings that kind of illumination. Sometimes it's extended quiet and a focused concentration on his attributes and qualities. Sometimes it's the discipline of praise, in which I deliberately try not to ask but rather to express, in my limited ways, my love and desire for God.

IT'S NOT JUST THE "GOOD BOOK," IT'S GOD'S BOOK. HIS VOICE IS IN ITS PAGES.

God isn't mute. He doesn't regularly speak from burning bushes, but he speaks nonetheless. When he wanted Moses to understand where the people were going astray, God shouted the commandments in a powerful storm that couldn't be mistaken. But more often, when we wrestle with deeply personal matters, he speaks quietly and soothingly. Scripture records it as his "still small voice" (1 Kings 19:12 NKJV). It's still and small for our benefit. It welcomes the brokenhearted. It's the voice of a loving father responding to the needs of a much-loved child. Speak to God by all means, but listen as well. He won't fail to reach the innermost parts of your heart.

You know that your ways have failed and you don't have the answers to life's most difficult questions. When you pray, you master the ability to accept God and his ways. Call it opening up to God, talking with your Father; it doesn't matter. What matters is the fact that you keep coming back to him. It's been said that when God wants to bless his people, he first moves them to pray.

Professor James "Buck" Hatch of Columbia Bible College used the example of an electric drill. He said, "The electric drill has the ability to work very efficiently when it's plugged in. But if you forget to put the plug in the socket, it has no power at all."[3] When you pray, you plug into a supernatural connection. The power is readily available and always on, but you must plug in to receive it.

> Draw near to God and He will draw near to you. (James 4:8)

4. WATCH YOUR FOCUS

If you look at the sun long enough, you'll go blind. Looking at your circumstances long enough may blind you as well.

I'm not suggesting denial. You have to confront the hard realities of your particular situation. But when you turn to God and ask for help, he shows you that your life isn't over. He has the compass, and he knows the way you should go.

The prophet Isaiah was told to deliver these comforting words to God's people: "Your ears will hear a word behind you, 'This is the way, walk in it,' whenever you turn to the right or to the left" (Isa. 30:21).

> GOD ISN'T INTERESTED IN YOUR ELOQUENCE; HE'S TUNED IN TO YOUR HEART.

From the first page to the last the Bible shows that it has always been God's intention to guide us. He has always been available to lead anyone who humbly asks for help. Perhaps the most important lesson of a lifetime is learning to ask—and learning whom to ask.

You say you don't know how to hear his voice. You're not sure where to find his guidance. Start with his Word, the Bible. No book has withstood more scrutiny. It's not just the "good book," it's God's book. His voice is in its pages.

After Moses died, the task of leading God's people fell to Joshua. Here's the direction he received from God:

> Be strong and courageous, for you will
> lead my people to possess all the land I
> swore to give their ancestors. Be strong
> and very courageous. Obey all the laws
> Moses gave you. Do not turn away from
> them, and you will be successful in
> everything you do. Study this Book of
> the Law continually. Meditate on it day
> and night so you may be sure to obey
> all that is written in it. Only then will
> you succeed. I command you—be
> strong and courageous! Do not be afraid
> or discouraged. For the Lord your God
> is with you wherever you go.
> (Josh. 1:6–9 NLT)

The way to stay focused is to stay in touch with
what God has said. We have been given a tremendous power—the power to choose. No matter how
hard it may be, we always have the power to decide
what we will focus on.

> For those who are according to the flesh
> set their minds on the things of the
> flesh, but those who are according to
> the Spirit, the things of the Spirit. For
> the mind set on the flesh is death, but

the mind set on the Spirit is life and
peace. (Rom. 8:5–6)

It's clear from these verses that each of us sets
our own mind. We have the power to control where
our mind goes. And the sooner we redirect our
mind, the sooner we'll be able to gain strength. You
may say, "I can't think about anything else, no matter how hard I try." Okay, I understand. I've been
there. But the truth is—you can. In my lowest
moments, I was always able to cry out to God. I was
able to pray—even if it was a rote prayer. In those
times, God isn't interested in your eloquence; he's
tuned in to your heart.

You can't bring back a loved one by extended
grieving. You won't recover a relationship or
become young when you're old by moaning about
what might have been. You don't heal a body by
shaking your fist at fate.

What is … is!

The saying "You can't change the circumstances, but you can change how you look at them"
has been repeated so often it has become a cliché.
It has been repeated so often because it's true.

Is it hard to force your focus off yourself and
how you feel? Absolutely. But does it help to do it?
Absolutely.

> The steadfast of mind You will keep in perfect peace, because he trusts in You. Trust in the Lord forever, for in God the Lord, we have an everlasting Rock. (Isa. 26:3–4)

It's hard work, but it has to be done. Turn to him and ask for his help. With understanding and compassion, he will help you focus on what's left, not what's lost.

5. REDEFINE SELF-WORTH

Self-worth is found in working your way past yourself. If you withdraw and live in sorrow and self-pity, you'll extinguish any sense of personal value. If you engage people and participate in life—even a little at a time—you'll begin to rediscover your value. Everybody has the potential to be valuable to those around them. Look outside yourself and opportunities will arise.

You have a circle of influence that includes family; friends; acquaintances; medical professionals; people at the coffee shop, newsstand, or garage; those in your church; and more. If you choose (and that's exactly what it is, a choice) to encourage those around you, your days will be full of meaning. You may not get a lot of thanks, and some people may not even notice or care, but that's not the goal. Your soul will be strengthened each time you give a little of yourself away.

In Romans 14:19, Paul writes, "Pursue the things which make for peace and the building up of one another." That verse contains God's definition of a role you can always fill. You can be a peacemaker, and one who builds up those around you. The enemy wants you to think there's nothing important for you to do anymore. His whole purpose is to tear down everything; he doesn't build up anything. God is focused on building up, and he shares that role with each one who's willing to accept it.

> HOPE IS THE FUEL ON WHICH THE ENGINE OF THE SOUL RUNS.

You're never too old or sick to become an encourager. You're never so out of touch that there's no one to build up. It's a role that has eternal significance, and you're the only one who can do it exactly where you are. You may shake your head and say, "How can I make any difference?" Don't confuse volume with value.

6. TAKE HOLD OF HOPE: AN ANCHOR FOR YOUR SOUL

In *Never Beyond Hope*, J. I. Packer recounts a story a wife told about her husband: "I shall never forget Francis' face as he walked through our front door that evening ... it was quite gray and utterly defeated. He'd been terminated without warning. Francis was then rebuffed everywhere. He was willing to do any work at all, but no one wanted him. It hurt me to see a man usually so full of vigor and ideas just silently helping me with the housework or sitting aimlessly staring into space." She continues that something happened to her husband while she was at a prayer meeting. "While we had been praying, he felt a change come over him. A spark of hope lifted him out of his despair. He was a different man when I got home. I do not know why Francis lost his job. But I do know that I can trust God. I do know that he will provide shelter and warmth and clothing and food. And he can give, even in the blackest moments, hope; and after faith and love, hope is one of his most precious gifts to mankind."[4]

Hope is the fuel on which the engine of the soul runs. For the soul to be purified and become holy, an ample supply of hope is necessary. Above all, God has always assured his people that there is reason for hope. The writer to the Hebrews put it this way:

> So that by two unchangeable things in which it is impossible for God to lie, we who have taken refuge would have strong encouragement to *take hold of the hope set before us. This hope we have as an anchor of the soul,* a hope both sure and steadfast and one which enters within the veil, where Jesus has entered as a forerunner for us. (Heb. 6:18–20)

An anchor keeps a ship from drifting and keeps it safe when storms blow. Your hope in Christ becomes the stabilizing factor and lets you focus on the ultimate outcome. It becomes the "anchor of [your] soul."

Hope is like a candle. One candle can light others without losing any of its own light. When you hope in Christ, you begin a journey from hope to hope, from grace to grace, from comfort to comfort, and "from glory to glory" (2 Cor. 3:18). Hope is a by-product of a relationship with God. It's a life-giving spring that flows from a never-ending reservoir.

This I recall to my mind, therefore I have hope. The Lord's lovingkindnesses indeed never cease, for His compassions never fail. They are new every morning; great is Your faithfulness. "The Lord is my portion," says my soul, "therefore I have hope in Him." (Lam. 3:21–24)

Martin Luther King, Jr., said, "If you lose hope, somehow you lose the vitality that keeps life moving, you lose that courage to be, that quality that helps you go on in spite of it all. And so today I still have a dream."[5] We find a source for this hope in the apostle Peter's words:

ACKNOWLEDGE THAT YOUR PAIN AND SUFFERING IS REAL, BUT DETERMINE NOT TO LET IT RUIN YOU.

Blessed be the God and Father of our Lord Jesus Christ, who according to His great mercy has caused us to be born again to a living hope through the resurrection of Jesus Christ from the dead, to obtain an inheritance which is imperishable and undefiled and will not fade away, reserved in heaven for you, who are protected by the power

of God through faith for a salvation
ready to be revealed in the last time. In
this you greatly rejoice, even though now
for a little while, if necessary, you have
been distressed by various trials, so that
the proof of your faith, being more precious than gold which is perishable, even
though tested by fire, may be found to
result in praise and glory and honor at
the revelation of Jesus Christ.
(1 Peter 1:3–7)

The words of the apostle Paul reflect this
thought, which is my prayer for you:

Now may the God of hope fill you with
all joy and peace in believing, so that
you will abound in hope by the power of
the Holy Spirit. (Rom. 15:13)

7. TAKE ACTION

Every day you choose to move forward or to
stand still. It's hard to get going and rebuild. In
fact, it's easier just to give up. But if you give up,
you dig a pit—and the longer you stay in it, the

harder it is to get out. In effect, by staying there you're saying that what you were before is all that matters. You're saying that if you are no longer what you were—an executive, a wife, a husband, a mother, in good health, or whatever else was the case—then you're nothing.

That lie can paralyze you and stop you from living. You're more than what you do. You're more than your roles and responsibilities. And you're more than what you were. As long as you're alive, God welcomes you to wake up each day and follow him. He will lead you out of darkness and despair and help you find the path of self-discovery, realizing that his feelings about you aren't circumstantial.

Acknowledge that your pain and suffering is real, but determine not to let it ruin you. God will help you, and he's the only One who can. There's nowhere else to go. Stop asking a "why" question and start asking God the "who" question:

"Who do you say I am now?"

That's when you begin the process of healing and restoration:

> "For I will restore you to health
> and I will heal you of your wounds,"
> declares the Lord. (Jer. 30:17)

"His-story"

But now, O Lord, You are our Father,
we are the clay, and You our potter; and
all of us are the work of Your hand.

—Isaiah 64:8

A wise old gentleman named Ivan Nelson once told me that all of history is "His-story."

"It's a fact," he said. "Life really is God's story, not ours." That point of view is echoed in *The Purpose Driven Life*. In that best seller, Rick Warren said it succinctly—"It's not about you."[1] In other words, there's something much bigger and more important going on here.

∾

IF YOU'RE NOT SURE WHETHER YOU HAVE ESTABLISHED A RELATIONSHIP WITH GOD THROUGH HIS, SON, JESUS CHRIST, YOU PROBABLY HAVEN'T.

"Whoever will call on the name of the Lord will be saved" (Rom. 10:13).

Now we've come to the most important part of this book, the part where you have an opportunity to come to know God personally. It's not complicated, but it requires honesty and humility. If you're not sure whether you have established a relationship with God through his Son, Jesus Christ, you probably haven't. There's an unmistakable assurance when you truly give yourself to the Lord. If you've never done that, or if you aren't sure, why not do it right now?

It's as simple as deciding that you truly want to know God intimately. If you do, open your heart to him and say the following prayer, then ask him to lead you to a church where you can learn about

the abundant and everlasting life he has in store
for you:

> Dear God, thank you for making me
> and for loving me, even when I have
> ignored you and gone my own way. I
> realize that I need you in my life, and I
> am sorry for my sins. I ask you to for-
> give me, and to cleanse me from all
> unrighteousness.
>
> Thank you for sacrificing your Son,
> Jesus, on the cross for me. I accept your
> gift of salvation purchased for me by his
> shed blood.
>
> Now I want to know you better. I
> want to follow you from this moment
> on. I ask you to come into my life and
> make me a new person. Send your Holy
> Spirit to live within me and to help me
> grow as a believer.
>
> Thank you for all that you have done
> for me in the past, all that you are doing
> for me in the present, all that you will
> do for me in the future.
>
> AMEN.

May this prayer be the beginning of the most important and most empowering relationship of your life. God bless you. Follow him. He alone knows the way:

I am the way, and the truth, and the life;
no one comes to the Father but through
Me. (John 14:6)

If you continue in My word, then you
are truly disciples of Mine; and you will
know the truth, and the truth will make
you free. (John 8:31–32)

EPILOGUE

Late September at Misquamicut Beach can be a little depressing. Anthony's and Paddy's are closed. The waterslides are dry. The batting cages are silent. The Surf Shop that sells shorts, T-shirts, suntan lotion, and boogie boards in the summer is dark. You can walk for blocks and not see a car in anyone's driveway. And if you've been here in "season" when the whole place is thriving—it becomes deafeningly silent by comparison. But I love it. In many ways, I love it more when it's empty.

I walk down Montauk and cross Atlantic Avenue. Just past Captain Zak's grill, I step over the chain that guards the empty parking lot. Approaching the dunes, I hear the roar of the ocean pounding a steady rhythm against the shore. It's a thunderous echo—crashing and rolling. Trudging through the sand in sneakers better suited to pavement, I make my way to the shore just where the receding waves have smoothed out the sand. The wet sand is packed tight, making it easier to walk.

> ℘
>
> WALKING THE SPARKLING COASTLINE, I REALIZE I'M A MERE GRAIN OF SAND ON ETERNITY'S SHORE— BUT I DON'T FEEL SMALL.

Except for a seagull or two, it's just the vast ocean and me. After a few moments of mindless meandering, memories begin to roll in on the breakers. I remember my son the day I was so down and he wanted more than anything to help me. I think of my daughter, at twenty, folding herself onto my lap and putting her head on my shoulder just to sit with Dad for a while. I remember my mother's brave offer to undergo a liver transplant if it would help keep me around longer. My mind settles on the way my wife, Dawn, sometimes grabs my arm and leans her head against my shoulder.

As I walk through the morning mist, I remember my sister and the look of acceptance that only she can offer. I see my brother and recall how he embodies all that was good about my days living at home before I went away to school. Walking the sparkling coastline, I realize I'm a mere grain of sand on eternity's shore—but I don't feel small. I feel blessed to be part of a much bigger reality. I know I'm part of God's plan. I'm satisfied with the good things in my life, and I accept the hard things I can't change. In my mind's eye I see faces of many of the important people in my life. I see couples I've had the privilege of counseling.

For a brief second, I have to laugh out loud as I think of my cousin Joe and how we can make each other cry laughing. My heart warms as I think of the strength I've seen in my cousins Donna, Lisa, Linda, and Maria—what a wonderful family I have. I see nieces and nephews who mean so much to me and who remind me of loving work I may yet do in their lives.

I walk alone, but I'm not lonely. The Lord is with me. He reminds me of many blessings. If his voice boomed off the waves and shouted, "Choose what you will focus on," it wouldn't be any clearer to me. I have to decide. I have the freedom to choose how I will live the remainder of my life. I'm a father, son, husband, brother, friend, uncle, cousin, neighbor, minister, and counselor. Nothing can ever change that. Who I am is who God made me to be.

I stop and turn toward the sea, and, with words from my heart, I pray, "God, give me the strength to focus on all that I have left and not on all that I have lost."

Amen.

READERS' GUIDE

*For Personal Reflection or
Group Discussion*

READERS' GUIDE

When life suddenly takes an abrupt and unexpected turn, what in the world are you supposed to
do? I'm not talking about an inconvenience or a delay.
I'm talking about a life-changing shift in your circumstances, something that turns things upside down and
leaves you disoriented and unsure of the next step.

This book was birthed in just such an experience. If you've experienced something similar, I
believe the things I learned can help. It wasn't a
straight line to recovering my balance and understanding how to go forward, but I did find it with

God's gracious help. I understand what you're going through, and therefore I've tried not to give you false hope. I've tried to stick with hope you can count on. It's my heartfelt prayer that you'll find comfort and direction in this book.

I invite you to use this study guide to dig deeper and see if you find helpful information. Although your circumstances may be different from mine, I humbly suggest that the things that helped me can help you. I believe that going through this study guide will help you uncover things that only God can reveal to you. May God bless, comfort, and strengthen you.

CHAPTER 1:
ONE CALL CHANGED IT ALL

1. Have you stopped to consider where your value as a person comes from? In this book, I try to explain that your "roles" in life don't define you. What are some things that contribute to a person's value (not job, position, title, or role in life)? If you are not sure, whom do you think knows your true value?

2. Healing takes place in the light, so begin to bring your hurt to the surface. What happened to you that turned your world upside down? It may be difficult, but try to be as specific and as honest as you can.

3. No one can handle alone something as hard as what you're going through, and neither can you. I know God can help. What are some of the ways you think God can help you in your situation?

4. What's the advantage of knowing your true self? (Not the self the world sees, but the self that God, your Maker, sees.)

5. Something in your life has dramatically changed. For a second, try to put emotion aside. In your heart of hearts, what do you think would be the wisest reaction to your circumstances?

Something to Consider

If God made you, and I believe he did, who would know you better than he does? Who would know the best way for you to recover and get on with your life? Take a few minutes to ask him to help you. Quiet yourself and sincerely ask him to help you get to know your true self, the self that's not contingent on others or circumstances or anything else. The self that God loves so much that he sent his Son to die for you. Despite the way you may feel, God looks on you and says, "Very good." Ask him to help you see yourself that way.

CHAPTER 2:
WHY START OVER?

1. You may be asking yourself, Why should I make the effort to start over? Think of three reasons and write them down.

2. A quote from this chapter reads: "The quality of your life is based on the choices you make." What do you think that means?

3. The chapter asks, "Will this choice bring me closer to where I want to go or move me farther away from it?" (Remember, doing nothing is a choice.) What does that mean?

4. Why is it important to be around positive, forward-looking people?

5. What's the difference between someone who handles major challenges well and someone who doesn't?

6. Do you know anyone who made the decision to start over? What are some good things that came from that choice?

Something to Consider

Take a moment and imagine your life one year from now. How would you like it to be different? Make a short list of the things necessary to bring about that change. Keep it where you can see it and remind yourself that with God's help you can look back in a year from a very different, and much improved, perspective.

CHAPTER 3:
THE MIND GAME ... IT'S NO GAME AT ALL

1. There are powers and principalities seeking your destruction. How does the Bible tell you to defeat them?

2. Whether you acknowledge it or not, there is a battle going on, and the prize is your mind. Why do you suppose the prize is the same for both God and Satan?

3. In 1 Thessalonians 5:8, Paul refers to a part of the armor of God as "a helmet, the hope of salvation." The connection between the helmet and the head is hard to miss, and the connection between the head and the mind is also obvious. Paul says our salvation is directly connected to our minds. Why is that?

4. It is clear in God's Word that willpower is not enough to win the battle for the mind. What else is needed?

5. How can God's Word be used as an offensive weapon in the battle for the mind?

6. Can the enemy overpower God's Word? What must he do when confronted with it?

Something to Consider

In Philippians 4:8–9, Paul says, "Finally, brethren, whatever is true, whatever is honorable, whatever is right, whatever is pure, whatever is lovely, whatever is of good repute, if there is any excellence and if anything worthy of praise, dwell on these things. The things you have learned and received and heard and seen in me, practice these things, and the God of peace will be with you." Paul says to "dwell on" these things and "practice" them. Those are active verbs that connote an ongoing process. How can you "dwell on" and "practice" these things?

CHAPTER 4:
CAN A CHRISTIAN BE DEPRESSED?

1. In Psalm 102, David describes his condition in terms that imply despair. Have you ever felt this way? What was it like for you? (Just hit the main points ... don't dwell on the negatives.)

2. If you have ever experienced any form of depression, what helped you get through it?

3. What role can prayer play in dealing with this problem?

4. Psalm 34:18 reads, "The Lord is near to the brokenhearted and saves those who are crushed in spirit." How can this verse help you in your struggle with depression?

5. Has God ever given up on anyone who asked for his help? Is any darkness greater than his light? Has he given up on you or removed his light from your path?

Something to Consider

If you're going through this kind of experience, take time to lay it all out for God. He already knows, but there's supernatural power in confessing every thought and need to him. The very act of praying focuses your attention on him, and that's always good. If you're not going through this kind of experience, take some time to pray for those who are. They can use your prayers, and in giving you will receive.

CHAPTER 5:
"I NEVER THOUGHT OF IT THAT WAY!"

1. If you had to describe yourself right now, as you read this, what would you say? If you used "role" words (mother, executive, widow), try again without using what you do to describe who you are.

2. Can God work through difficult circumstances? Why is it that he sometimes can work more effectively through us when we're going through great pain?

3. If you made a list of five or six people who love you, who would be on that list? Do you invest energy in your relationship with those people? (If you have no friends or family, there are people in churches all over the world just waiting for the chance to get to know you and love you.)

4. What do you think life is really all about? Who is the very best expert on the subject? What does he say about life?

5. How much does your view of life affect your behavior? Why?

Something to Consider

Just for a minute, suspend reality and pretend you're God. As you look at yourself from his perspective, how would you counsel you? Share with the group or write it down to study by yourself.

CHAPTER 6:
"WHO, EXACTLY, DOES GOD SAY I AM?"

1. Have you ever been at a gathering (reunion, wedding, etc.) where you ran into people you haven't seen in a long time? What are some of the first things people ask each other at these events?

2. If people you haven't seen in a while ask, "How are you?" do you give them an account of your activities or tell them something personal about yourself? Why?

3. How do you suppose God evaluates who you are?

4. Opinion without knowledge often adds up to false conclusions. Have you ever been incorrectly judged? What did it feel like? Have you ever judged someone else incorrectly based on a false impression?

5. Is it possible to judge yourself incorrectly? What can you do to avoid or correct that mistake?

6. You're not important because others say so. You're important because God made it so. How does that fact affect your idea of who you are?

Something to Consider

In Psalm 139:13–14, the psalmist wrote of God: "For You formed my inward parts; You wove me in my mother's womb. I will give thanks to You, for I am fearfully and wonderfully made; wonderful are Your works, and my soul knows it very well." Spend some time in prayer asking God to help you understand why he made you. Open yourself to the comfort of his Word. Pray for the grace to see yourself through the psalm quoted above.

CHAPTER 7:
WHAT WILL YOU SEE IN THE REARVIEW MIRROR?

1. When you're gone, what will people remember about you (good and bad)?

2. What is keeping you from doing something about the bad?

3. Sometimes being vulnerable and allowing others to help you can open the door to deeper relationships. Why is that?

4. Why is it such hard work to understand what's really important in life?

5. What do you believe is your life's most important work? How does that work affect the impact you have on others?

Something to Consider

How would you like to be remembered? How can tragedy or hardship shape what people will remember about you?

CHAPTER 8:
"WHAT DO I REALLY BELIEVE?"

1. What you believe about the experience of life shapes how you live it. Why is that?

2. Why is living for others' approval a dead end?

3. Do you believe your life can have meaning again? Do you believe you can use your painful experience to comfort someone else? Why would it be important to do that?

4. Do you believe God cares about the outcome of your life? What does that mean to you?

5. What shapes your belief system?

Something to Consider

Take a few minutes and discuss or write out what you really believe. Ask yourself if your core beliefs are in line with where you want to go and who you want to be. If they aren't, what would you have to do to develop some that are?

Chapter 9:
Relationship: The Key to Self-Worth

1. Why are relationships so important to human existence?

2. There are tons of so-called "relationship experts" out there. Why hasn't any one of them been able to come up with a definitive guide to relationships?

3. Our society often tells us to look out for number one. How is that a relationship killer?

4. How do you build a loving relationship with God?

5. You are made to be in relationships. What do you suppose happens when you choose to withdraw from all relationships?

Something to Consider

Why do you suppose Jesus said that love is the greatest commandment of all? Can you love in isolation? If you said yes, then explain how. If you said no, explain why.

CHAPTER 10:
CONSIDER IT ALL JOY ... WHEN YOU SUFFER.
YEAH, RIGHT!

1. Do you think anyone should learn to enjoy pain? Why or why not?

2. Does it say (anywhere) in the Bible that pain is good? Where? Does it say (anywhere) in the Bible that pain can be a teacher or an instrument of learning? Where?

3. Ecclesiastes 12:11 says, "The words of wise men are like goads, and masters of these collections are like well-driven nails; they are given by one Shepherd." (*Webster's* says that a goad is a long, pointed stick used for prodding cattle and other animals or something used to motivate somebody or stir someone into action.) How can a hard circumstance be a goad?

4. Why is it important to take an honest inventory of your circumstances?

5. Everything in life is in a constant state of change. What does that tell you about preparing for changes?

6. What did the apostle Paul mean when he wrote, "When I am weak, then I am strong"?

Something to Consider

Discuss a time in your life when pain brought gain. What was it like when you were going through it? What is it like now looking back on it? Could you have learned the things you did if you hadn't gone through it?

Chapter 11:
"Is There No Balm in Gilead?"

1. Why is recovery rarely a straight line?

2. How do you weaken yourself when you withdraw?

240 I HAD OTHER PLANS, LORD

3. Why is it so tempting to try to escape from your problems?

4. Why is it always a dead end to try to escape from your problems?

5. How does withdrawing affect the people around you?

6. Have you ever heard people testify to God's help in their life? How did they experience that help?

Something to Consider

Bishop T. D. Jakes, on one of his monthly messages sent out to supporters, preaches a message entitled, "It only works if you drink it!"[1] He is talking about the "rivers of living water" Jesus promised to the woman at the well (John 7:38). Jesus offers these same rivers to each of us today. What do you think "It only works if you drink it" means?

CHAPTER 12:
IT'S REALLY UP TO YOU

1. Your future is always in your hands. Why is that?

2. Why do some people stay locked up in a prison of self-pity?

3. How is not making choices a choice in itself?

4. Why do people want to feel in control? Is control an illusion? Why?

5. Why is it important to give control to God?

6. What was the prophet Jeremiah talking about when he delivered God's question: "Is there no balm in Gilead?"

Something to Consider

Spend some time in prayer on this subject. Ask God to help you understand his provision. Ask him to increase your faith in his ability to supply all that you need. Consider the fact that it breaks his heart when you don't take advantage of the help he offers.

CHAPTER 13:

STARTING OVER: SEVEN SUGGESTIONS
TO HELP YOU GET GOING

1. Why is it hard to ask for help?

2. What happens when you humble yourself and ask God for help?

3. Discuss the fact that good consequences can and often do come from bad circumstances.

4. How does prayer help in the healing process?

5. Why is hope absolutely essential to recovering from a difficult circumstance?

6. Discuss the fact that you never get anywhere by standing still. Why is it important for you to take steps—even small ones?

Something to Consider

Sometimes God reveals only the next step. Why is it important to take each step as it comes and not jump over the next step? How do you know what the next step is?

Chapter 14: "His-story"

1. Who created everything you see and experience? What does that tell you about life?

2. Do you need to understand "everything" about God to believe in him? Why or why not?

3. Why does God want to help you through your difficulty?

4. Why is your perspective on life critical to recovering from hardship?

5. Using only positive terms, answer the following questions: Who am I now? Who do I want to be? Where do I want to go? What's the best way for me to get there?

Something to Consider

Knowing that God completely understands you and all you've been through, form your own prayer asking for his help. He respects free choice and won't force himself on you. You must ask him to help you. His help is the key to recovery, healing, and hope.

NOTES

Chapter 2

1. Joni Eareckson Tada and Dave and Jan Dravecky, *NIV Encouragement Bible* (Grand Rapids, MI: Zondervan, 2001), 791.

Chapter 4

1. National Institute of Mental Health, http://www.nimh.nih.gov/healthinformation/depressionmenu.cfm.

Chapter 5

1. David O. McKay, Hearts & Minds, http://www.heartsandminds.org/quotes/selfexam.htm.

2. Robert S. McGee, *The Search for Significance: Seeing Your True Worth Through God's Eyes* (Nashville: W Publishing, 2003), 53.
3. Ibid.

Chapter 6
1. Dr. Chris Thurman, *The Lies We Believe* (Nashville: Thomas Nelson, 1989), 66.
2. Scott Larson, "The Significance Snare," *Rev! Magazine,* May/June 2000, 65–69.
3. Oswald Chambers, *My Utmost for His Highest* (Grand Rapids, MI: Discovery House Publishers, 1935), 262.
4. William Shakespeare, *As You Like It,* act 2, scene 7.

Chapter 7
1. Max Lucado, *A Love Worth Giving* (Nashville: W Publishing Group, 2002), 160.
2. Elizabeth McKenna, *When Work Doesn't Work Anymore* (New York: Delacorte Press, 1997), 43.
3. Ibid., 43–44.

Chapter 9
1. Joseph Stowell, *Perilous Pursuits* (Chicago: Moody Press, 1994), 13, 21.